YOUR HOME
YOUR MONEY
YOUR FUTURE

Since eighty-five out of a hundred women will
spend part of their lives alone, it is important to
understand how to make your money do the most
for you. In WOMEN AND MONEY, Mary
Rogers, a respected financial advisor, offers sound
tips and solid approaches for every area of the
financial spectrum.

"Informative, easy-to-read . . . a good primer for
women who want to learn financial responsibility"
Chicago Tribune

"Comprehensive . . . a variety of basic subjects
including record keeping, budgeting, using credit
wisely, insurance, investments, retirement programs,
wills, and estate planning . . . first-rate material
on the merits of term life insurance, the pros and cons
of tax shelters, and the advantages of joint-tenancy
arrangements. . . . Perhaps the authors' greatest
service to their readers is equipping them to deal with
accountants, attorneys (divorce or estate), brokers,
and other professionals. . . . Eminently
useful for every woman's home."
Kirkus Reviews

WOMEN AND MONEY

MARY ROGERS & NANCY JOYCE

AVON
PUBLISHERS OF BARD, CAMELOT AND DISCUS BOOKS

AVON BOOKS
A division of
The Hearst Corporation
959 Eighth Avenue
New York, New York 10019

First Avon Printing, September, 1979

For CAM *who gave me the courage*
to be Mary Rogers

Contents

		PREFACE	9
Chapter	1	WOMEN AND MONEY	11
	2	MONEY MANAGEMENT	27
	3	INSURANCE	46
	4	INVESTMENTS	68
	5	REAL ESTATE	91
	6	TAX SHELTERS	106
	7	RETIREMENT	116
	8	DIVORCE	124
	9	DEATH	139
	10	THE WOMAN ALONE	158
		APPENDIX	165
		INDEX	169

Preface

It is my hope that this book will prevent any woman from finding herself old, alone *and poor*. Every woman must assume the responsibility for her own financial future by becoming involved, as early as possible, with the management and planning of her family's finances. Most families just mush along through their earning years, with no plans for their current or future financial needs. They arrive at the day when the last paycheck comes in expecting a miracle to happen, some unknown force that will provide the money that is needed to support a wife and husband for fifteen or twenty years after retirement. Unfortunately, there is no miracle.

Every woman must face the fact that she is probably going to be alone at some time in her life, either because of death or divorce. The woman who keeps her head in the sand and doesn't face reality may find herself alone and poor. This doesn't have to happen. All women have the ability to understand finance and manage money. In fact, because women are intimately involved with the day-to-day financial needs of their families, they are able to see the need for money management and are supremely suited for the role of family financial manager. I think women should view their families as a business, one that someone must oversee and make plans for meeting today's and tomorrow's needs. If you assume this responsibility, alone or with your partner, everyone in the family will benefit—you, your husband, and your children. Everything you do to insure a secure financial future for yourself will also make life better for your family. You only have one life to live, and I want you to enjoy every minute of it. I don't want any woman ever to have to live in a back room of a dingy hotel or have to move in with her children because she can't afford anything else. Life can be golden, but it doesn't just happen, you have to make it happen.

M.R.

Tiburon, California
March 1978

"MY WIFE HAS NEVER WORKED..."

Chapter One   # Women and Money

Why does a book on finances have to be written for women? Because most women are one step away from welfare and don't know it.

Women and Money is three books. It is the personal story of Mary Rogers—housekeeper, wife, working mother—and her attempts to create the good life for her family on an average income. More important, it's a book for and about all women. And last, it's a book about money, a basic primer on money management and family financial planning.

Let's take a look at some statistical facts about women. Projections from the U.S. Census Bureau state that of 100 typical American women now 21 years old, 6 will never marry; of the 94 who will, 33 will see their first marriage end in divorce; of the remaining 61 who stay married, 46 will outlive their husbands. Thus, 85 out of 100 women will be on their own at some time in their lives.

These are not just numbers out of some government study, they are facts that affect all women. Ask yourself some questions right now. What if my husband doesn't come home tonight? What if my husband should die at 60 and I live to be 80? Do I know where I stand financially? Do I know what it would cost to maintain my present standard of living?

The average income for women over 65 is well below poverty level, a sobering fact we all should consider. At some point in every woman's life she is probably going to be alone, and her financial situation at that time will depend on how well she plans today. Women must take responsibility for their financial futures. It is no longer realistic to assume that your security is taken care of simply because you are married. I'm sure that many of the women who find themselves alone and poor were told they didn't have to worry, that everything was taken care of. The risk is too great—you can't afford to assume anything, you must know where you stand.

Being alone does not have to mean financial disaster, but unless you have confronted the reality of possibly being alone and have prepared for it, you could find yourself and your children on welfare. When a wife dies very little happens to the husband financially, but when the husband dies all hell breaks loose for his wife. A man still has the ability to earn money, that ability is not taken away. He owns his pension, profit sharing and the like, and the credits he has built up in Social Security. He can usually maintain the same standard of living.

For the woman who hasn't taken responsibility for her financial future, the picture is not as bright when her husband dies. Generally, she has been out of the work force for a number of years and is ill suited for finding a well-paying job. She may receive the small amount of money her husband had placed in his pension plan, but not the full amount of the pension. She is eligible for Social Security benefits *only* if she has a minor child and only until that child is 18. After that time she won't receive any more payments until she is 60 and even then the amount is not as high as her husband would have received. If her husband had any life insurance, the amount she receives depends on the type of policy he had. It could be a nice lump sum or it could be a pittance.

Scary? Yes, but you see, Mother never earned any money. The record shows that Mother never worked.

My Wife Never Worked

A man once told me, "Mary, my wife never worked." I blinked and thought to myself, I think I'll look into this a little further. This is what I found out:

Louie and his wife Sophie lived in a small town. When they were married, Sophie went to live with Louie and his parents on the family dairy farm. The morning after the honeymoon, she went out to help milk the cows. As time went by she had three children and raised them while working for Louie's family. Then World War II broke out and Louie joined the Army. Sophie assumed more of the responsibilities on the farm and somehow managed to save enough money to send the three children to college.

When Louie came home from the war he said, "Boy, Sophie you're doing such a great job with the farm, why don't I go into town and work at the factory?" So, Louie worked at the factory during the week and helped run the farm on weekends. After Louie's parents died, Louie inherited the farm. The children married and left home and Louie retired from the factory.

Somewhere there is a record of the time Louie served in the Army and another record of the years he worked in the factory, which entitles him to a pension for his lifetime. And then there is a Social Security record, showing that Louie should receive a Social Security payment for the rest of his life, and finally, there is a record in the County Clerk's office that shows that Louie owns the farm.

What about Sophie? There isn't a record anywhere that shows that she ever did anything. "My wife never worked," said Louie. Many of us are in the same boat. Up until now, no one has been able to put a price on a wife and mother's labors. She may not hold down a full-time job and earn a salary, but she certainly works as hard as her husband, keeping house, cooking meals, running errands, raising children, etc.

If there is a divorce, it can mean financial catastrophe for both partners. Rarely is a man's income adequate to support two households in the style to which each partner has become accustomed. Seldom are divided assets sufficient to maintain the house you once shared. Bleak, yes. Hopeless, no. If you know where you stand financially and know how to make every dollar work for you, being divorced or widowed doesn't have to mean a drastic change in your lifestyle.

I've just subjected you to the potential horror story facing every woman. We all know a friend or relative who has been through it. It's no surprise to any of us, but for some reason we play deaf, dumb, and blind when it comes to ourselves. It's time to stop playing games with your life. It's the only one you have.

The Last Paycheck

What about the possibility that you won't ever be alone? Most families spend more time planning their annual two-week vacation than they do planning their financial futures. Most people are what I call "pass-throughs." They accept the paycheck at one end and they just pass it through and pay all of it out at the other end. Nothing stays with them. Nobody saves. Everyone goes blithely along, pretending there is no end to this money. Well, think again. Even the Ford Foundation has a limited amount of money. There is a limited amount of money a person can earn in a lifetime and it has to do three things: support you now, possibly help your children, and support you for ten to twenty years after you receive the last paycheck.

"Oh no," you may say. "My husband says that he is not going to retire. He likes what he is doing and so he is going to continue working." Don't try to fool yourself. There is a last paycheck.

Why not eliminate all the guesswork? A little money management and a little financial planning will not only enable you to achieve short-term goals (paying off the car, making needed house repairs, etc.) and long-term goals (funding your children's education and providing retirement income), but also will let you know what there is left over to enjoy now.

In my experience, family crises arise over extravagance by one partner, at the expense of essential savings or necessities, while the other partner goes without a luxury long dreamed of. Full partnership in responsible family planning should include equal sharing of the toys we all crave. The joy of spending is one more dividend of responsible family financial planning. In fact, it's what earning money is all about—saving a little now, getting it to grow, and then having the enjoyment of spending it at the right time.

I feel that women are the most logical family financial managers because they spend most of the family income. They are familiar with the family's immediate needs and they are also the most vulnerable member of the family if financial mistakes are made. Financial management and planning are not that complicated, not some mystery that only an Einstein can figure out. We can all add and subtract. It isn't our brains or lack of them that is a problem, it is the way we have been brought up.

We've come a long way from the days when a husband could buy, sell, borrow, and commit his family in financial matters without consulting his wife. Co-responsibility in family financial transactions is slowly becoming the norm in most states. Do you know what co-responsibility means? It means that you are equally responsible for everything you sign. If you co-sign a loan agreement for $20,000 and your husband dies, that loan is still your debt. Yet most women are still programmed from the past to remain ignorant and rely upon men for making their financial decisions.

Father Knows Best. Or Does He?

It seems that from the time most of us were little girls we were taught that men should make all financial decisions. In the past this may have been proper. Men received an education and most women didn't, so perhaps Father (husband, brother, son) did know best. This isn't the case today. All women are educated. (Even if they were told to steer clear of those "nasty" male subjects like Math!) We must learn to overcome our past programming and also help men to overcome theirs.

Men are not the "enemy." The enemy is our past programming. Men have also been locked into old patterns. They too follow their father's footsteps. They are trained to be the providers, the money machines, and they think they should know all the answers. Maybe, just maybe, they need some help.

The world of money is constantly changing. Old laws

are constantly being revised and new laws are formulated. For instance, does your husband know that Federal estate, death, and gift tax laws were changed in 1976? Does he know what changes are likely to occur in income tax laws in the near future? If he doesn't, someone should, because these laws will affect your family's finances, now and in the future. To prepare for these rapid fluctuations in the world of money, to plan for the future with reasonable provisions for what could happen, a husband and wife must work together as equal partners in financial matters, just as they do in other areas of the marriage partnership. When you stop to think about it, most wives who don't work full-time outside of the home have more time to research the family's next financial move than their busy husbands.

Today the average man is working eight, ten, or twelve hours a day. It's a dog-eat-dog world out there and he is probably so busy earning money that he might not have time to plan what to do with it. When he comes home at night he's exhausted. He doesn't want to talk about family finances then and he doesn't want to talk about them on weekends either. If there is going to be any kind of family financial management program, it might be up to you to start one.

You have the time, the energy, and the brains to take the burden off your husband's shoulders. You can do it better than anyone else can. Do you have any idea of how good you really are? Your volunteer efforts are the heart and backbone of this country's cultural activities and charitable organizations. You are the greatest fund raisers, researchers, and shoppers around. Money couldn't buy the talents and expertise that the women of this country possess!

Every time you go to the store and look for the best buys you are practicing money management. Every time you set aside a little money for that dress you know your daughter wants for the prom, you are practicing money management. This may seem like a gross over-simplification, but I assure you that total financial planning for the family is exactly the same thing, only on a larger scale.

Many women don't like the idea of initiating a financial plan. They consider it a man's responsibility. It just doesn't seem feminine. This is pure nonsense and I hope to convince you of that.

Some of you have husbands who will be taken aback by all this talk of money. They will say, "What do you mean you have a financial plan for us?" "Haven't I always taken

care of you?" "Don't you trust m
the time, you really don't have t
may be shocked when you say, "
really am interested. I would li
finances."

Just remember that this attitude is
sticky situation and you may have to
under it. The point is not to get all fir
the door and say, "John, from now on
care of everything!" Let your husband kn   at you appre-
ciate all that he is doing for you and the kids, but that you
are interested in helping him make your lives together the
best they can possibly be.

Your marriage is a partnership and you are both working
very hard, putting out equal amounts of effort to make that
partnership work. It is important that you let your husband
know that you trust him implicitly, that you are not trying
to take over, but that you feel you should know and understand the family's finances and that you think you might be
a big help to him.

I Can't Talk to My Husband About Money

Talking to husbands about money seems to be the one
area that can strike terror in the most outspoken of women.
Why do husbands and wives lead isolated financial lives?
If I've heard it once, I've heard it a thousand times: "I can't
talk to my husband about money. He thinks I'm just a spendthrift, he doesn't trust me with money." Why does he think
that? I know that some men may feel terribly threatened,
but I get so tired of hearing about it. I also think we're exaggerating the situation.

When a husband holds all the financial information to
himself it must be for one of three reasons: one, he's so conditioned to traditional patterns that it has never entered his
mind to think of you as a financial partner; two, he remembers your financial irresponsibility in the past and he is afraid
of a repeat performance; or three, he is covering up something he doesn't want you to know about. It's up to you to
find out what the problem is and try to solve it.

Take a good, hard look at your particular situation and
be honest about it. The problem may have started so long
ago that you may have forgotten about it. Take, for instance,

...ng gal who called me one day in a state of ... "Mary, please come and talk to me. My hus-...nding all of our money!"

...t Margaret for lunch and the whole story came tum-...ng out. Margaret was upset and angry because her husband Ed had sold a piece of property and she thought he must have made some money on it. She didn't know what Ed had done with the money and she wanted to buy a new sewing machine. Well, that was quite a beginning! I asked Margaret if she knew how much money her husband earned. She wasn't sure of the exact figure, but he had recently increased her monthly allowance. Then I asked if she knew what he spent his money on. She didn't know. Margaret was completely in the dark about the family finances. How did she get herself into this position?

Margaret came from a family where her father had assumed full financial responsibility for the care of his family. Her mother lived on a monthly allowance, and was told that father would take care of everything. If anything happened to him, their friend Jim would manage the family's finances.

How was Margaret going to learn anything about money? She had followed the pattern set by her mother and accepted her family's money arrangement as normal. During the first few years of Margaret's marriage, she made some frightful mistakes, bouncing checks and using credit cards recklessly. She was extravagant with money and had no idea what Ed's financial situation was. Ed was appalled by Margaret's behavior and made up his mind right then that he couldn't trust Margaret with money. So, for the past fifteen years he has given her a monthly allowance—enough to buy groceries and a little extra spending money. He also allows her to charge some clothing to his accounts, but for the most part, his control has been absolute.

Now, at 37, Margaret realizes that she knows nothing about money, but she resents being treated like a child. In digging deeper, I found out that Ed *had* been planning for their future. He had set money aside for the children's education, and had even started a fund for their retirement. None of the money from the sale of the property had been spent, it had all been carefully invested.

What about Margaret? She wanted to be an equal partner in the family finances, but she was going to have to earn that right. She had to move slowly, a step at a time, to show

Ed that she was capable of handling money, that she had at last broken out of the mold of a helpless wife.

Many of us are going to have to do the same thing to show well-meaning husbands that we are capable of accepting some responsibility for the family's finances. Each one of us has an individual barrier to overcome. We must look at the situation honestly and decide the best way to scale that barrier.

For some of you it will be easy. John might just say, "Fantastic, honey! You know I haven't had time to think about what we should be doing with our money. I can sure use your help." But, whether it's easy or tough, remember that you have no choice in the matter, you must learn. So, don't give up, you'll find a way to do it somehow.

Now, you've got your foot in the door, and you've let your husband know you're interested. Where do you go from here? First, you have to find out what your present financial situation is. You can't manage your money, and you can't plan what to do with it, unless you know how much you have to work with.

Keeping Records

The first step for every financially responsible woman is to become "Keeper of the Family Records." The important thing to remember about keeping records is that there is no one way to do it, but family records should be clear enough so that anyone other than you who may need to refer to them can understand them instantly.

If your husband is already taking care of the family records, there is no need to duplicate his work, but you should become familiar with his books so that you understand what he is doing and learn to share in it. In some instances your husband's secretary may know more about your family finances than you do. I think this is absurd. Learn to ask questions.

The Mary Rogers Financial Records Book is a loose-leaf binder that holds standard-size ledger sheets which can be removed or replaced. This book is not only a record of what we own and how we spend our money, but also is a reference tool for all our financial planning.

Putting together your own family financial records book takes time, but once you get all the fundamental information down on paper you'll find that it is not difficult to keep up to date. Once it is complete, you can pick up that book and say, "Here it is, the complete financial story of my family." (Chapter 2 will explain exactly how to put your book together.) You are ready to start working toward your financial goals. You are ready to start planning how to achieve those goals. You are ready to start researching ways to make your money work for you.

There are many choices available, everything from savings accounts, stocks, and bonds to income real estate. You should investigate all of these choices and then decide what investment possibilities are realistic for your family.

I'm sure that many of you are thinking, "My God, I don't know how to research investments! I wouldn't know where to start." Never fear. The purpose of this book is to introduce you to financial terminology so that you know what questions to ask and where to go for answers. It is meant to provide you with a basic knowledge of taxes, insurance, investments, pensions, etc. The information you will get from this book will not make you an authority on finance, but it will help you to understand it and be able to deal with it.

Setting Goals

Before you decide what you want to do with your money, you have to determine what your goals are. I'm talking about realistic goals, not pipe dreams—although those are nice too! There are BIG goals that lie further down the road and there are smaller goals that ultimately will yield the BIG ones.

My first goal was to save $100. It may not sound like much, but for me it was almost two months' income. Also, at the time of my planning, we had recently come out of the Depression and were in the middle of World War II, so extra money was scarce. Well, it took me quite a while to save that $100. My next goal was to save $1,000 and that was a little easier. I found that having a little money in the bank meant more to me than spending money on small luxuries. These little goals were leading up to a biggie—a downpayment on a "vine-covered cottage" that Cam and I had our heart set on. When our son John came along, we started a small savings account for his education, and a few years later we started saving for Cam's retirement. You would be amazed at what the miracle of time did to all those small savings.

It sounds as if we did nothing but scrimp and save so that ultimately we could be old and rich. Not true! I don't believe in living shabbily today to save for tomorrow. One of my top goals was always to live as nicely as we possibly could, but to keep a balance between our present needs and our future requirements.

You and your husband must decide what you want that requires money. For example, you might decide you want a two-week vacation every year; a college education for Susie and Tommy; and a retirement fund for your future. After you set your goals, you have to determine how much money you are going to need to fulfill them.

Let me digress for a moment. Many people have asked me how inflation will affect their savings. I don't know the answer to that question. As I mentioned earlier, the world of money is constantly changing. I grew up during the Depression and we had nothing. A dollar went a long way in those years, so those of us who grew up in that period became conditioned to protect ourselves against the next depression. We hung onto every dollar that came our way. In time we realized that the recurring current crises were not potential depressions, but rising inflation. The dollar didn't buy as much as it used to, so we found that each dollar we saved would have to earn a lot more money to cover our requirements. So, you see, you can't predict what the economic situation will be like forty years from now. However, the person who saves and plans will be much better off than the person who doesn't, regardless of the situation in the future.

Now, back to how much money you need to achieve your goals. The biggest priority on your list should be building a retirement fund. But if this is your first excursion into financial management, it will probably be difficult to start tackling a goal such as your retirement. I think you should start with a small goal such as saving and planning for your next vacation. This is an easy goal to achieve, and the reward of a prepaid vacation has a little more reality than saving for retirement, which might be twenty years away. Working on a short-term goal will help to keep you on the right track, and the habit of saving and planning will slowly become more and more ingrained in your daily life.

Estimating your monthly retirement needs is a little more

complicated than determining the cost of your vacation. You need to decide how much money you'll need to live on each month. Also find out the exact amount of any automatic retirement income you would receive from Social Security or Federal and State retirement benefits, your husband's pension, or fringe benefits. You should examine this fixed monthly income from two angles: the amount you'll receive if your husband is alive and the amount you'll receive if he dies. The Social Security office can provide you with charts that tell you exactly how much monthly income you'll receive at a certain age. The information about your husband's pension plan can be obtained from his employer.

There are hundreds of computers, working twenty-four hours a day, spewing out financial plans for individuals. Every insurance company and investment company can provide you with a detailed computer printout—usually at no charge—that will suggest the path to follow to meet your goals. Far too often this information is obtained, but little happens unless a persistent salesperson insists that you take some action.

For the sake of simplicity, let's start out with a realistic goal of having $100,000 in some good investment by the time your husband retires at 65. At least shoot for it. You may be amazed to find that it is possible to save this much if a small amount is put away each month and you don't spend the earnings of this investment.

I think of financial planning as buying a couple of hens and a rooster. I feed them well, let them do their thing (in financial jargon this is compounding), but I never eat the eggs. I am building a flock. When we retire, we will start eating the eggs and at some point we may even eat some of the chickens.

Once you have a goal, where do you put your money so that it will have the greatest return? Basically, there are three things you can do with your money: you can put it in a savings account (a must, because you need to have immediate access to cash for unexpected expenses and also for your short-term goals); you can loan your money; or you can buy something with it for future growth.

A savings account is self-explanatory and at today's rate it will probably earn around 5 per cent annual interest.

Where can you loan money? You loan money when you make investments. For example, you loan money to the government when you purchase savings bonds. One thing to remember is that there is some risk involved with everything you do with money. Generally, the higher the risk, the greater the possibility of earnings or growth. You must evaluate the amount of risk you are willing to take. Remember, there are many investments that will fit your needs, but there is no "perfect" investment for all of us.

Perhaps you want to buy something. Why? Because you think that what you buy today will increase in value. You might also buy something as a tax shelter for some of your income. Whatever the reason for buying, you will find that there are many things you can buy that can potentially give you a profit on your investment. Some possibilities are: land/real estate or stock ownership in a company. (I will expand upon all of these investment possibilities in Chapters 4 and 5.)

In the course of researching what you have and what you might like to have, you are going to have to ask hundreds of questions, and you are going to have to learn to talk to professionals. By professionals I mean attorneys, personnel officers, stockbrokers, insurance agents, accountants, and so on. You have to talk to them to find out where you stand financially and you'll probably need to talk to them in the course of researching investments.

Most women are afraid to ask stupid questions. All they have ever heard is, "Trust me. It's just too complicated for you to understand." Or "Why do you want to know?" And the final, "I don't have time to explain, just sign here." We get it from husbands and we get it from the professionals too. Well, we've put all that behind us. We know it's not too complicated and we realize that we can't afford to be in the dark. We also always hear, "Don't worry, Jim will take care of everything if anything happens to me." Of course, Jim could die too, but perhaps your husband hasn't thought of that.

I want all women to be aware of the value of using attorneys, accountants, and other professionals, but these people will be of no value to you unless you know what questions to ask. I want you to use these people, but I want you to make your own decisions. I don't want you to go in as the helpless woman who says, "Do what you think is fair." This has been the case all too often in the past and it's time to change all that.

What questions do you want to ask? The source of many of the questions you will ask will come from your family records book (detailed in Chapter 2). To simplify things here, I'll list several questions under the heading "What every woman should know":

1. What do we own? How does it work?
2. What portion of my husband's profit sharing fund or pension do I receive in the event of his death?
3. Am I the beneficiary of my husband's life insurance? Would I continue to be in the case of divorce?
4. Do we own a safe deposit box? What are its contents? Where is it located?
5. What Social Security benefits am I entitled to?
6. What do we owe? To whom? What interest rate are we paying?

Those questions are just for starters. Now let's look at some more questions and I'll label these "What every couple should know":

1. When do we want to retire?
2. What monthly income will we need after the last paycheck?
3. What amount of money will be needed for our children's education?
4. Will financial help be needed by elderly parents?
5. Are our assets well balanced between those that can quickly be converted to cash and those that cannot?
6. Is our plan flexible? Can it be modified as goals change and income fluctuates?

These are fundamental questions, but how do you go about getting answers to them? The logical place to start is with your husband. More than likely, he has the paper work on all of your assets and liabilities. Get it. Read the material and see if you can understand it. If you don't understand it, ask your husband or decide who among the professionals you need to talk to. If you find that neither you nor your husband understand his pension plan, call the personnel officer of his company and make him explain it to you—in your language.

I know it's not as simple as it sounds. All of us have been put down and made to feel our questions are silly. We are reluctant to ask the questions that have to be asked. We go into an attorney's office, or an accountant's office, or a stockbroker's office and they may talk way over our heads while we sit demurely and try not to look totally baffled. We don't force them to stop. We don't say, "Wait a minute! Talk to me in my language so that I can understand what you are saying!" Until you start saying this, they will continue to ignore you and continue to put you down if you ask something which to them may seem stupid. I am convinced that most of the talk is a snow job anyway!

The first time you behave this way it'll be rough, but if you want to be a financially responsible woman, you have to learn to talk to the professionals. You cannot afford to remain a nonentity. You have to know what you are signing before you make any commitment. The object is to open up some doors, either very gently or with a small kick, in order to learn and understand your finances and become a real partner in your marriage.

There is another aspect of financial planning that I'd like to mention. Being an obstructionist is not productive. You can't arbitrarily decide, "No, I'm not going to sign." You should have a good reason for not wanting to sign a document and should always maintain a flexible attitude.

Once you know where you stand financially, you can figure out how much "extra" money you have, and make some short-term and long-term goals. Then you have to decide where to put that extra money so that it can grow. Once you've done all this you can present your proposal to your husband.

The first rule in financial management and planning is *never* talk about money in the abstract. Talk about money with a piece of paper and a pencil. Don't shout through the bathroom door while George is shaving. Don't try to talk about money when the TV is blaring and the kids are playing "Cowboys and Indians" all over the house. The response you will get from George will be anything but encouraging! Pick a quiet time when you can sit down, with a paper and pencil, and present your idea. If your idea is down on paper, it will be much easier for George to understand it.

You've probably spent a lot of time and energy on your idea, and naturally you think it's the greatest thing since pantyhose, but George just might not think so. Remember, you are equal partners but you won't always agree. So don't get discouraged. You've worked hard and you've learned a lot. Right? And you're probably feeling rather cocky. I understand—I've been in that position myself.

When I showed Cam my first financial proposal, I'd been in training with a brokerage house for a year and I mean to tell you I was so impressed with Mary Rogers—there wasn't anybody as good as I was! I thought I was so smart!

Well, it was a little embarrassing to find out that I didn't have all the answers. Nobody does, so don't be a smart alec, fall back and regroup. If you really think it's a good idea and your husband hasn't given you any valid reason why it wouldn't work, put it on the shelf for a while. It'll still be there a couple of weeks from now. You've planted the seed in his mind; it may grow yet.

I began this chapter by forcing you to look at the reality of being a woman. I tried to scare you and I hope I did. I wanted you to face the fact that you will probably be financially alone one day, but I also wanted you to realize that it doesn't have to mean disaster. You'll never know the terror of waking up one day and having to ask, "What will I have to live on?" You'll already know. I hope you've also begun to realize that by becoming financially responsible you've added a new dimension to yourself. You and your husband will become true partners because you will be sharing another facet of marriage.

I think that every woman whose husband brings home a paycheck should take it upon herself to manage that money so well that when he brings home that last paycheck, she can proudly produce the results of her efforts—a pot of gold, a gift to both of you for all those years of hard work. Wouldn't that be nice? I think it would. My fondest hope is that the following chapters will help every woman towards a more responsible and therefore happier life.

THIS IS A LIST OF EVERYTHING I SPENT MONEY ON TODAY.

Chapter Two   # Money Management

Financial planning, management, and goals are all terms that we've heard many times. They are abstract concepts that will never have any real meaning until you and your husband try to fit them into your lives. First you should have goals, then you should plan how to achieve those goals, and finally you should learn to manage your money well so that the plans can be carried out. It sounds fairly simple, doesn't it? Well, we all know that it's not.

All of us, at some time in our lives, have thought about different things we'd like to have—a new car, a trip to Europe, a second home, etc. These goals should be well thought out. They should be realistic goals, ones you can achieve. Most important, they should be highly desirable and mutually satisfying to both partners, otherwise, you won't have the incentive to achieve them.

The planning phase is directly related to management. If you can manage your money well, you will have the funds to plan with. Some women scoff at the idea of money management and think it's a waste of time. One woman told me that she didn't have to worry about financial planning because she was going to inherit money. It sounded great, but I decided to do a little research to find out exactly what her inheritance amounted to. She did inherit some money, but all of it was placed in a trust and her monthly income from the trust only amounted to $500—barely enough to cover her monthly expenses.

I have heard so many stories about people who were counting on an inheritance for their financial future—a grandmother who said she would finance the children's education, but when dear old grandmother died there was less than $1000 in her estate. I think each one of us should accept the responsibility to save and fund any future expense—education, retirement, etc. Then if there is any money left after mother or father or grandmother dies, it will come as a pleasant surprise. The cost of care for the elderly can consume large sums of money quickly and there may be nothing left over to give. Play it safe—do your own planning and saving.

Many of you might find my methods of money management a bit extreme (and sometimes crazy!), but I hope they will give you some ideas you can incorporate into your own financial scheme. The first question I asked myself when I started to think about money management was, "What do I really want out of life?" The answer was easy. I wanted the "good life" for my family—a nice home, good food, vacations, the works—and I was willing to do everything possible to achieve that goal.

I've found that the biggest hurdle in money management is being completely honest with yourself. We all tend to play games with ourselves. We act like an overweight person on a diet. When we are around other people we are soooo good, but as soon as we're alone, watch out! Let's stop playing these silly games—we're only hurting ourselves. We all know when we've spent money foolishly. It's a shame to waste money when you could be putting it to work for you.

If you stopped to think before you spent money you would realize that you waste at least $10 a week on odds and ends that amount to nothing. If you put that $10 a week in a savings account earning 6 per cent interest, your money would grow to $30,000 in twenty-five years. That $30,000 nest egg is much more satisfying in the long run than all the junk that $10 a week could buy. It's the little spending that usually consumes the greater part of your income. You're too tired to cook, so you go out to the local hamburger joint for dinner. It's usually more expensive than eating at home, it's not that good, and you don't even have a fond memory of a special evening out. It may seem like a small amount of money, but this kind of spending adds up quickly.

As a young wife who wanted the good life, I decided to find out exactly where all our money was going. For an entire month I wrote down every penny I spent. I found out that my small spending was adding up to big amounts. That very moment I made a decision that changed the course of my family's life—for the better. I wasn't going to spend 29 cents ever again, because 29 cents didn't buy anything I really wanted. I was going to save all those wasted 29 cents and let them grow to $29. Then I would be able to buy something of value. If you think I'm overdoing it, find out for yourself just how much your little spending is costing you. Write down every cent you spend for one month and I think you'll be in for a nasty surprise.

It's hard to condition yourself not to spend little amounts of money. I found that a reward system worked best for me. I forced myself to stay away from fast food places and then a few times a year Cam and I would really dine—candlelight, fourteen waiters, and wine with every course. These meals became fond memories. Of course, eating out is not the only danger zone. There are hundreds of other pitfalls. I happen to be addicted to those fabulous little stores that sell the most beautiful inexpensive junk. I can spend $50 in ten minutes on all kinds of cute little things that I don't really need. I avoid these stores like the plague all year, but on my birthday I make a beeline to my favorite and have a ball. During the rest of the year ten horses couldn't drag me there.

I spend cautiously. I do a lot of planning and thinking before I let loose of our money. I try to buy value. I want to have things that will last a long time or else nothing at all. I refuse to hire someone to do something I can do myself. If I can't do it myself I hire someone, but never because I'm too lazy or I find the chore distasteful. Whenever I hear of someone who has recently hired a gardener or cleaning woman, my mental calculator clicks on and I find myself adding up what that money would amount to over a certain number of years and I end up knowing that I'd rather work a little harder and have the extra money.

Yes, I watch my pennies, but I don't go overboard. I have learned the mistake of driving all over town to save a bit on a purchase; the cost of driving will far exceed my savings. Just because it's SALE DAY I don't go tearing down to the store, because I know I'll probably end up buying something I don't really need, simply because it's on sale. Store owners aren't dumb; they know that once they get us in the store our resistance is at half-mast, so they have all those enticing sale items lined up and waiting. There are exceptions, of course. If I've already decided that I need a certain item and know that it will be sold at discount at certain times of the year, I'm the first one in the store.

One of my pet peeves is spending money on necessities. Buying necessities isn't gratifying. Whenever I buy a necessity I make sure it lasts as long as possible. I take good care of everything. I don't want to have to replace an item any sooner than I have to. I like luxuries. I'd much rather have my household savings spent on a new love seat than on a lawn mower and a garden hose!

Many people have told me I'm crazy, but I think it really boils down to not having false pride. I never really cared what other people thought about me and at times I've done some pretty funny things. My son John will probably never forget my wood scavenger days back in the fifties. We lived in a nice track home development and because of skillful money management we were the only family on the block with a fireplace and a Cadillac. I did some research on car prices and found that we could buy a two-year-old Cadillac for the same price as a new Ford, so we bought the Cadillac. We had this great wood-burning fireplace and we needed firewood. I noticed that on garbage day the neighbors would put all kinds of burnable wood out on the curb to be carted away, so every Wednesday John and I would drive that big Cadillac up and down the street, filling up the trunk with wood. Poor John, who was about 8 at the time, would be scrunched down in the back seat hoping that no one would notice that he belonged to such a nutty woman. We had some great fires and some great laughs at John's expense, and it didn't cost us a dime.

You may wonder how all of these little savings relate to the big money that we all need for long-term goals such as retirement and college tuition. It sounds as though I'm advocating saving money so you can buy luxuries. This isn't true. I want you to be aware of the choices you have. You can choose to live modestly most of the year so that your vacation is the highlight of the year or you might choose to give up your summer vacation to pay for a year of college. What are your priorities? How do you want to spend your money?

It wasn't long ago that most people didn't have any choice as to how they spent their money. All of their income was needed to pay for the basic necessities of life: food, clothing, and shelter. This is usually not the case today. It is estimated that one-third of the average family's income is discretionary. That means it is not needed to keep a roof over your head and clothes on your back. What you decide to do with this money is up to you. You can piddle it away on junk or you can use it to fulfill your goals. Perhaps a certain portion should be spent on luxuries you want now and the rest should be socked away for tomorrow. If you manage your money wisely, you'll have enough to do both.

The Mary Rogers Financial Records Book

True money management starts with finding out exactly how much it costs you to live and becoming aware of where all your money is being spent. If you know both of these facts, you can achieve control over your spending. This brings us to the Mary Rogers Financial Records Book that I mentioned briefly in the first chapter. This book should contain your family's complete financial history. I have a book for every year, dating back to 1941 when Cam and I were married. Much of the information in each of these books is repetitious, but it's important that all your financial information be kept in one place. This book is for your own use now, but it is also for whoever may need to see your records in the future. If you and your husband are killed in a car accident, someone is going to need to know your financial history. There is nothing worse than having to root around in back closets and dust-covered file cabinets to try to find a family's records. If your records are scattered about, your children and other loved ones may suffer because of it. Make it easy on yourself and whoever else may need to know your financial history by keeping records up to date and in one place.

As I've mentioned before, it doesn't make sense to talk about money in the abstract. You have to put figures down on paper before you can begin to get a clear picture of your financial situation. Money can be one of the greatest sources of family arguments, so if you write everything down you'll know exactly what you've spent and where your money is going. You can't argue against the figures on a piece of paper. Fight the paper, not each other.

I want you to know where you stand financially. I want you to have a record of your day-to-day spending habits, so you'll have a clear picture of where your family's money is going. From the records you keep you'll be able to find better ways to manage your money and decide upon a financial plan that will best help you achieve short- and long-term goals.

In the process of putting together a family records book you will learn a tremendous amount about your family's finances and I think you'll begin to realize, as I did, that it really isn't the amount of money you make that counts, but the way you manage it.

Keeping Records

There is no one way to set up your records. Any number of different methods will work so it's up to you to determine the one that is easiest for you. There is, however, a list of basic information that every record book should contain. I find that a loose-leaf binder with ledger paper works best for me because I can insert pages as I need them.

The first, and perhaps most important item that goes into my record book is the information from my checkbook. All of my spendable income is deposited into my checking account. On every deposit I make a note of where that money came from: a paycheck, bond interest, a dividend, etc. I also keep a detailed account of every check I write: who the check is made out to and what it paid for. When I pay my credit card bills, I don't just list the total amount I paid, I list each purchase by category—such as clothing, gasoline, etc.—so that I have all that information available when I list it in my check register. I don't write checks for little everyday expenses, I write one check for cash that will carry me through until the following week. I keep track of those cash expenses by noting them in my checkbook. If I have a joint checking account and my husband is also writing checks against the account I ask him to give me a listing of all the checks he writes and what they cover. This may not seem like much to ask, but some husbands might think that you're prying into their business and be reluctant to give you the information. If you hit a snag like this, just explain that you're not being nosey, you're simply trying to find out where all your money is going so the two of you can make some sound financial decisions based on that information. Don't make a big issue of it.

A couple of times a year, when I have a quiet time to myself, I get out my checkbook and transfer all that information to the check register pages of my record book. It may seem as though I'm simply duplicating information, but I'm making a permanent record and I don't want to have to rely on boxes of checkbook stubs that can easily get lost or misplaced. These pages look exactly like my checkbook—they tell me where my income comes from and where I spend it.

At the end of the year I copy the remaining information from my checkbook into my check register pages. Then I pull out all the check register pages and group all of our expenses under separate categories. I list the amounts by category, such as clothing, food, rent, utilities, insurance payments, car payments, medical expenses, home repairs, gifts, vacations, etc. After I add up the totals for each category I know exactly where all our money went. Now when my husband brings home his W2 form (record of his annual wages) and asks where all the money went I can show him. There is no guessing, no argument. It's all down there in black and white. Once the figures are down on paper we can see what our major expenses have been for an entire year and can determine if we need to cut back in one area or another. We may find that it's time to buy a new car because the cost of maintenance and repairs on the car we now own has become too expensive. If we know where our money is going, we can learn to budget more wisely.

Budget is a word that often scares people, because they think it means cutting back to bare necessities and following complicated guidelines. Who wants the restrictions of a budget? I think that a budget can be very beneficial. A new widow or divorcee who hasn't had the experience of managing money is often frightened to death by new financial responsibility. By making up a detailed list of her anticipated expenses she can determine whether she has the income to meet those expenses. Once she can see that her expenses and income balance on paper then she can relax and set up guidelines for spending. It's the person who refuses to write down how money is spent who will constantly be afraid because she doesn't know what is happening to her money. A piece of paper and a pencil can solve this problem.

Financial textbooks often discuss budgets by breaking down your total income into recommended percentages for food, shelter, clothing, transportation, etc. Actually, budgets should reflect the personal requirements of your family. No two budgets are the same. A family financial records book is a personal record that reflects your family's lifestyle, so no two books will be the same either.

Your book can contain any information you want, but here are a few guidelines you might find helpful. I include a complete history of every member of my family. I traced my own history first, listing the schools I attended, the jobs I've held and the salary I earned from each one (yes, I did remember), places I've lived and traveled to, etc. This took a lot of time to research and put down on paper. I followed the same procedure for my husband Cam and our son John. This is also an ideal place to note information about your children: childhood diseases, shots they've had, academic and athletic achievements, graduations, and so forth. You can keep all your records together in one book.

Our financial lives are full of documents and numbers and the information on the documents should be recorded in your book. These documents include birth certificates, marriage licenses, divorce decrees, adoption papers, automobile titles and registration, veteran's papers, insurance policies, last will and testament, etc. The documents themselves should be kept in a safety deposit box in a bank. The list of numbers should include the following: Social Security numbers, employee identification numbers, checking and savings account numbers, credit card numbers, and safety deposit box numbers (along with the location of keys and a list of the contents of the box).

Your records book should contain a financial statement, listing everything you own and everything you owe. This will require a little research on your part to get all of this information in order. If you are just starting out, don't be surprised if you owe more than you own—it's quite natural. Most young couples are in the same position.

Insurance policies are especially important. You should keep a page on each policy, detailing the coverage it provides. Most people have policies for life insurance, health insurance, fire insurance, and auto insurance.

You should have a written account of every real estate transaction you've made, for tax purposes. I went back to the escrow papers for each house that we've owned and copied all the information from the papers into my records book. I wrote down what the house cost, the name of the escrow company, the number of the escrow, and the date the deed was recorded. The entire history of each transaction is in my book. Then I went back to my records and found all the bills and checks paid for any improvements to each house, such as the brick patio we laid, the new cupboards we installed—anything that improved the property. Improvements are different from maintenance costs (if you replaced an old water heater, it is not considered an improvement). Why did I go to all this trouble? Because for every house we sold at a profit I added the cost of improvements to the original cost of the house, thereby reducing the amount of profit that we had to pay taxes on. (This is covered in detail in Chapter 6—Tax Shelters.)

I also happen to be a receipt freak. On January 1, I designate an empty drawer in my desk as my receipt drawer. During the entire year I collect every receipt as if my life depended on it. At the end of every week, my purse is chock full of paper and I dump every receipt into the receipt drawer. I make a note on the receipt so I can remember the items I bought. I don't bother filing anything—I make it as simple as possible for myself. I know I have a receipt for everything I've spent, even a bridge toll.

What do I do with that drawer full of bits of paper? Well, the first week of January of the next year, I pull out the drawer, sit on the floor, and start sorting receipts into little piles. One pile for gas bills, one pile for rent or mortgage payments, one pile for insurance payments, and so forth. Most of my receipts go into the fireplace. Why did I keep them in the first place? Well, I never know when I'll have to refer back to a receipt. If there is a question about whether I paid an old bill or if the balance is correct, I have the information at my fingertips.

Some of those piles are important. I have a large envelope marked "Tax Information" and some of my piles go into that envelope: interest earned, interest paid (such as credit card finance charges, which I hope you don't have), medical expenses, donations to charity, taxes paid, etc.—in short, all those items you need for tax deductions. I check these receipts against the information I have in my records book to make sure they agree and then I'm all done. I may never have to refer to that "Tax Information" envelope again, but it is a backup of information for itemizing deductions on tax returns.

Following this system, by the end of the first week in January you have most of the information you need for your income tax return. You may have to wait for your employer or bank to give you information on your income and interest earnings, but otherwise you're ready to go. You can be first in line for your refund, or, if you owe additional money, you know how much you have to save before that April 15th deadline. More important, you know exactly what you've spent and how.

What about all those cancelled checks for the year? I sort these into piles also. My criteria for keeping a check is whether I'll need that check to prove a bill was paid. I keep all cancelled checks and receipts for taxes paid, debts paid, etc. If you make a big purchase such as buying real estate, a car, or a boat, or if you loan money to someone, keep your cancelled check. It can prove that the transaction took place.

In one of my classes, a woman told me that her mother-in-law had asked her to pay in cash the monthly payments on a loan she had given her. This is crazy! How can you ever prove that the loan was repaid? In repaying personal loans to friends or family, it is especially important to keep the cancelled check of any payment made. I can see the situation now—your mother-in-law dies and someone in the family remembers that she loaned you and your husband money for the down payment on your house. Since there is no record of repayment, they decide to deduct it from your share of the estate. You'd better have proof that you repaid the loan or it could cause problems. You may think this could never happen in your family, but there is no sense in playing with fate. Have some proof!

How long should you keep cancelled checks and receipts needed for tax purposes? The Internal Revenue Service (IRS) can only call you back for records that are three years old, which actually means four years if you count the current year in which you are filing. I suggest you keep backup records for five years just to be safe. Some records you'll want to keep forever, but don't weigh yourself down with a lot of unnecessary paper.

Your book should also contain a record of all your investments, such as stocks and bonds. Each investment should be listed, even those that you've sold, because someday you may be questioned about one of your investments and you'll have to prove what you did with it. I suggest that you write down the reason you made the investment at the top of the page: for income, future growth, or whatever. I think this is important because people often forget the initial reason for making an investment. If you write down the reason, you can evaluate the investment from time to time to make sure it is fulfilling its original purpose. If it isn't, you may decide that it's time to sell.

You should have a record of all profit sharing and pension plans, including a detailed explanation of all the benefits. What is the true story about that pension? What amount of money do you receive and when? How much are you entitled to if your husband dies before he retires? If he dies after he has retired, what happens to you financially?

I found out that if my husband died before he retired, the only thing I would receive was the group insurance that covered him as an employee and the amount of money that he had put into his retirement account, not the full amount of his retirement benefits. It was a shock to realize that the amount Cam had contributed to his retirement fund was a mere pittance compared to what his pension benefit would be if he lived. So, in actuality, the only money I could count on was the amount of money we had saved and owned in both our names.

There are three basic methods of paying pensions. You can choose one of the three at the time of retirement. The first type is based on the wage earner's (say your husband's) life span, which means that he will receive a pension for as long as he lives. When he dies, the payments stop. This type of pension pays the highest monthly amount of the three plans. The second type of payment plan is based on the wage earner's lifetime or ten years certain, meaning that the pension will remain in force as long as the wage earner is alive and it guarantees that the monthly payments will continue for ten years after retirement if the wage earner should die. This means that if your husband should die five years after he retires, his estate (you or your children) will receive retirement benefits for five more years. If he should die ten years after he retires, then you will receive nothing from his pension plan.

The third type of pension payment is based on the life span of both husband and wife. It pays less than the first two plans because the pension will continue until the last partner dies. When husband and wife are close in age reducing the benefits is not too painful, but if their ages vary greatly, this method is rarely advantageous or practical.

Anything that I, my husband, or our children have inherited is listed in my book. For example, I inherited a small estate from my father when he died, so I have a complete record of the cash, house, and stock he left me and the amount of State inheritance tax I had to pay. The complete transaction is fully described. Why? Because some time in the future, at my death or my husband's death, the State/Federal government will need to know where the money in our estate came from, for tax purposes. Did it come entirely from wages, did we inherit money, and so forth?

All current bills, notes, installment contracts, and loans should be noted in the records book and it's also a good idea to keep copies of your most recent income tax returns.

Another important thing to keep in your records book is a complete inventory of your home. I sat in my living room and wrote down everything in the house and put an approximate value on each item. When I have a chair recovered, I make a note of it because it increases the value of my chair. If there is anything in my house that is extremely valuable, such as original art, I make sure I contact my fire insurance agent about it, because if it isn't covered by our policy, I won't be able to collect on it. I suggest that you put a copy of your house inventory in your safe deposit box so you won't lose it if there is a fire or theft at your house.

Putting together a financial records book takes time, but once you get all the basic information down on paper you'll find that it isn't difficult to keep up to date. Keeping track of where your money is going will help you establish a budget. Once you see where waste is occurring you can determine how to save that money. Your records book is essential for making any financial plan.

I look at my spending with an eye on the entire year. There are many expenses that are not monthly, such as insurance premiums, property taxes, school tuition, vacations, Christmas, etc. I know when these expenses will occur, so I plan for them. I total all these one-time costs and then divide them by the twelve months of the year. Every month, I set aside in a savings account what that monthly amount would be. This way I spread the cost over the entire year. I have peace of mind and those bills aren't the burden they would be if I didn't plan for them. When the bills come in, I move money from my savings to my checking account and write the check. It is just one of the many ways that you can maintain control over the spending of your money. There should be no surprises.

I am always looking around the corner. I can remember when John was little and all the little boys in the neighborhood had dress suits, which they usually wore once. I decided to forgo that pleasure until John graduated from high school and I would buy him a tailor-made suit. Well, it wasn't tailor-made, but we bought it from his father's favorite shop and he looked as handsome as I had dreamed. This is one example of deciding how and when you want to spend your money.

This kind of "penny pinching" was occasionally hard for John to understand but I wanted him to know the value of a dollar. Sometimes this wasn't easy because we did live very well. We lived in a nice home, drove nice cars, etc. and John was no dummy. He knew we weren't poor. One day John came rushing home to tell me he wanted a new bike called a derailer. What on earth was a derailer? Well, it was a super bike with gears and all kinds of nifty little features and it only cost $120. I was in a state of shock! I couldn't believe that a bike could cost $120 and I immediately started making negative noises. John looked me in the eye and asked me what kind of car was sitting in our garage. I answered, "A Cadillac," and began to see his point. You can't fool children. They have an unerring ability to see things as they really are. You can not say one thing to them and do something else. They will see through you.

Lack of money can cause terrible anxiety. If you practice wise money management, you will find that you have enough money to live comfortably now as well as in the future, particularly during your retirement years. You can eliminate the anxiety for you and your husband. You will never face retirement wondering where all your money went and what you will have to live on. This is especially true for the years when you'll probably be without your husband.

The key to security is saving money and making it grow. The biggest mistake people make is waiting until they get a big sum—$5,000 or whatever—before they do anything. That day never comes. You don't need a big lump sum to start saving money. There are many places to invest small amounts of money—banks, savings and loans, mutual funds, etc.—that will ultimately yield the larger sums you'll need to invest in the things that will bring you bigger returns.

You don't need a lump sum to invest, but one way to acquire a lump sum quickly is by never living on two incomes. In fact, this is how Cam and I got where we are today. When most people get married, they are both working at full-time jobs. If they plan to have children, it's usually a couple of years in the future, so you have at least two or three years with both partners as wage earners. Unfortunately, many couples choose to spend both incomes. Wouldn't it be wiser to live on one income and bank the other? Even if the woman's income is not as large as her husband's (as is often the case), it could amount to thousands of dollars in a couple of years. That's a sizable nest egg and it was exactly what Cam and I had. Even in later years when our son was in school and I held a part-time job, we never cashed any of those checks. They all went into our investments. That money was our future and we never touched it.

If you are just starting out your life together, this is an excellent way to save money, but if you've passed that stage of your lives, you must find other ways to stockpile your money. Look at every money transaction with an eye toward value. Am I stretching our money as far as it will go? Is there a loophole somewhere that I can close up? The Mary Rogers spending philosophy is really a game—making a nickel do the job of a dime. It's a great challenge and I have a lot of fun trying to win the game. Some people react to this as being limited and poor. They don't enjoy the game.

Using Credit Wisely

A modern-day phenomenon that can eat up your money faster than you realize is credit cards. We live in a credit society. We can buy anything on credit, but the only reason credit is available to us is because someone is making a profit by providing that service (lending money). There probably isn't a person reading this book who hasn't at some time gotten in over her head by buying on credit.

I'm not sure that I agree with the recent advertisements that advise young couples to borrow money to establish credit. I still don't go along with the idea of paying more for interest than you are making on your own investments and savings. If you can show an increasing balance in your savings account, and the prudent use of credit cards, then you are establishing a good credit record without paying large sums of interest needlessly.

When you use credit cards foolishly you are borrowing money at the highest interest rates around. I find credit cards very convenient, but I use them only when I KNOW that I can pay the entire balance due when I receive the bill. By doing this, I am able to borrow money from department stores and other lending institutions for free (there is no interest charged when you pay the bill immediately), while my own money (that I will ultimately use to pay the bill) is earning top interest elsewhere. When handled this way, credit cards can be very useful. You can get something for nothing and earn money at the same time. From what I understand, however, some credit card companies are considering charging a fee for their cards (several do already). If this happens, I will go back to paying by check or even (heaven forbid) cash.

The Truth In Lending Act states that every lending institution that charges interest or finance charges must inform you of their annual interest rate. Most major credit card companies list their annual rate at 18 per cent, broken down into a monthly rate of 1½ per cent. Just out of curiosity I decided to check this out, so I left a balance of $100 in my account to see how much interest I would be charged. I expected it to be $1.50, based on the monthly rate of 1½ per cent. Was I in for a surprise when my next statement arrived, showing that I owed $3.13 in finance charges.

Well, I went back over my bill and reread the statement about annual interest rates. It was then that I noticed the line about "Average Daily Balance." The finance charges were based on the average daily balance in my account, including purchases not yet due for payment. What a sneaky way to do business! I was being charged interest on some items I had already paid for and some for which I hadn't been billed. By using this average-daily-balance system my credit card company was charging me a lot more than 18 per cent annual interest. I multiplied the $3.13 finance charge by twelve months and found that I was being charged an annual percentage rate of 37.5 per cent. This is out-rageous, but unfortunately, it's also perfectly legal. Why haven't people yelled about this? Because so few people pay any attention to the interest they are charged. Look over your bills carefully and see how the finance charge is determined. It's one more rat hole you can plug.

Another credit card trap is that little item called "Mini-mum Payment Due." In many instances it's only a little more than the interest charges on your account and if you only make the minimum payment you'll never get out of debt. This is exactly what the credit card companies want, because the longer you take to pay off your debt the more money they'll make on interest charges.

People play games with themselves and many of my clients have boasted that they are saving all kinds of money because they have an automatic monthly withdrawal from their checking accounts into their savings accounts and/or credit unions. These savings are earning 5, 6 or even 7 per cent annual interest. Well, that's just marvelous, but at the same time they are using credit cards to make purchases. They are living in a fantasy world. They may be saving large sums of money, but as a result they don't have enough money (cash) to pay for the things they need. Their savings may be earning 6 per cent interest, but their purchases are costing them 18 per cent and more. It's better to put a little money aside that is a true savings than to play the credit game.

Another little self-deception game is what I call "When is a bargain really a bargain?" When you buy something on sale and pay for it with your credit card you may end up paying more than the original price of your purchase if you pay your bill in monthly installments. This is crazy!

Credit cards are great, but use them wisely. Remember it's the small spending that makes the difference in money management, and finance charges mount up quickly. I refuse to pay finance charges, unless it's for a big emergency, but if I'm the money manager I think I am, there will be few emergencies that I can't handle. Sometimes we are all forced to borrow, but I borrow at the best rates available and not at 18 per cent or higher.

One of my goals is to keep a balance of $1,000 in a savings account at all times. This is for my peace of mind. If the transmission on the car has to be replaced or the water heater bursts, I won't have to borrow money to pay the bill.

When I do have to borrow money I use my assets as collateral so I can get the best interest rate on a loan. If you have any stocks or bonds you can offer them as collateral to get a lower interest rate. You still own the stocks or bonds, and you still receive the dividends or interest they pay, but you can't sell them until your debt is paid in full. If you don't pay back the loan, the bank or other lending institution can sell the stocks or bonds to get back the money you owe. You insure your own loan and therefore the bank can offer you a lower interest rate. You could have sold the stocks or bonds to pay for what you needed, but this would defeat your long-term goal by decreasing your assets. It's a much better idea to keep them and make them work for you. It also forces you to live on your income, not on your assets.

Another type of credit that I favor is borrowing money to buy a home. Getting a mortgage is a great way to borrow and save, but make sure you shop around for the best interest rates and the least point charges for establishing a mortgage (covered in detail in Chapter 5—Real Estate).

Your monthly mortgage payment is one of the best saving disciplines around, because come hell or high water you usually find the money to make that monthly payment. You are paying interest on the loan, of course, but you are also building up ownership in your home. Part of your monthly payments goes toward paying back the principal of the money you borrowed, the rest is the interest. A mortgage is particularly valuable for the family that finds it hard to save money. The cash equity you build up in your home is very much like a forced savings account.

You can also use your home as collateral in order to borrow more money, by getting a second trust deed or second mortgage against it. For example, if you bought your house for $50,000 and it's now worth $100,000 you can arrange to borrow on the increased value of your home. This is usually short-term borrowing of five to ten years. If you sell your home before you've paid back both mortgages (your original mortgage and the second one), the lenders will take that unpaid amount out of your selling price. It's nice to know you have this source of ready cash, but I think it is unwise to tap it unless you have a real need, such as a medical emergency.

The main point I want to stress is that you should investigate all your possibilities before making a financial decision. Every financial transaction has a hidden cost—sometimes it is well hidden, but it's there. Fnd out what the cost is and see if you can eliminate it. This is an important facet of money management.

Loaning Money to Friends or Relatives

The opposite of borrowing is loaning. In most cases loaning your money is an unemotional, profitable business transaction (discussed in Chapter 4—Investments). There is, however, a type of loaning that is emotion-charged and in my opinion unwise: loaning money to your children, relatives, or friends. You may think that I am wandering from the topic of money management, but I'm not. Money management involves every financial decision you make. I believe you should never loan money to children, relatives, or friends that you can't afford to give outright. Money between family members should be given with no thought of repayment. If it's paid back, fantastic, but if not, then no one gets hurt. Emotions and money don't mix and generally result in poor financial decisions and poor money management.

A dear little lady in one of my classes expressed shock when I said I thought lending money to children was unwise. "My goodness," she said. "That's exactly what we're doing right now—lending money to our son George to help him with the downpayment on a house." I asked her how the money was going to be paid back and how long they were giving George to pay back the loan. "Well," she said, "we hadn't talked about that yet." Then I asked her how much interest they planned to charge George. She wasn't sure, but she thought it was about 6 per cent. There had been no thought given to this exchange of money as a financial transaction. Dad would probably write George a check and that would be that.

Once George moved into his house he would probably need to buy things to fix it up nicely, so he'd have to charge things—furniture and so forth—at department stores and building supply stores. If George is as smart as I think he is, he would want to pay off those debts with high interest rates before he pays back his parents' loan at a low interest rate. What parent wouldn't agree with George and let him delay the payments? I don't want this type of situation to arise. Loaning money to an individual is the highest risk you can take, and people with limited funds should never get involved in this kind of transaction. You're just asking for trouble. What would I do instead of lending money to George? I would give George any amount that I could afford to give, with no strings attached, no repayment necessary, and I would enjoy that gift.

Helping your children is great and we all want to be able to do it, but your help should be a gift you can afford, not a debt. One thing I hear frequently from parents that drives me crazy is, "Unless I loan them the money, they'll never be able to own their own home." This simply isn't true. If your children want a house bad enough, they will find some way to get the money together. Why take the chance of destroying something that is worth much more than money? Helping your children should bring you pleasure, not emotional upheaval.

Another situation where I feel money and emotions don't mix is what I call "Lovers Make Lousy Lenders." A close friend of mine, who was recently divorced and had a cash settlement in the bank, became involved in a romantic relationship. She and this new man in her life spent a wonderful weekend together, touring the wine country of northern California. They ran into a small winery off the beaten track, and after a little wine tasting they started talking about how much fun it would be to invest in some land in the Napa Valley. There was some land nearby that had an old house on it that could be fixed up and they even knew of a man who could manage a future vineyard and winery. The whole idea seemed about as romantic as one could get. That night my friend and her newfound love put together their ideas on paper and made plans for their future investment. When she told me about her plan I was aghast and told her I thought it was one of the most foolish moves she could make. No matter how good the investment, you should avoid getting involved in a business deal with a lover (excuse me—romantic friend). When the passion cools, the money transaction could be a weight around your neck. One partner would always want out before the other and this would cause nothing but trouble. A business deal is a business deal and it should never be clouded with emotion.

Money management should become a part of your lifestyle rather than be an occasional thought or action. Although you may not realize it, it invades every aspect of your life, from the clothes you wear to the car you drive, the house you live in, and the food on your table.

Chapter Three   Insurance

Next to the phrase, "it's tax deductible," insurance is probably the most frequently misused and misunderstood term in the family's financial repertory. What is insurance and why do we need it?

To boil it down to its most basic element, insurance is a group of people getting together to share the loss of a catastrophe. In olden days, if our neighbor's barn burned down, we all got together to build a new barn. We all contributed our labors to overcome our neighbor's catastrophe.

Today we have insurance companies that act as holding agents for all of us to share a loss. We can now determine statistically how many houses are going to burn down this year; how many fenders will be bashed in; how many people will enter a hospital; how many people in different age groups will die this year; and so on. The price of insurance is based on these estimated incidents of loss. Of course, the cost of insurance must also cover the insurance company's overhead and guarantee them a profit too.

This overhead and profit factor is one aspect of insurance that I want to emphasize. Insurance companies (and their agents) are not philanthropic enterprises; they are out to make money just like everyone else. Remember this the next time you talk to an insurance agent. He is out to *sell* you something and you can be sure that he will try to make the biggest commission possible on his sale. Before you buy, find out exactly what someone is trying to sell and decide which type of insurance best suits your family's needs.

What kinds of insurance do you need? There is insurance available for almost everything you own—from your toes (if you are a ballerina) to your Picasso—but you cannot insure yourself against all disasters. It's simply too expensive. You have to decide what your greatest risk areas are and distribute your insurance dollars accordingly.

Insurance is a necessity and a vital part of every family's financial planning, but there are a great many misconceptions as to the choices available. You probably already have insurance on a variety of things so the place to start is in researching what you already own. Find out what kinds of insurance you have and what each policy covers. Then decide if the insurance you own really fits your needs.

Most of us are aware of the need for auto insurance to cover us in the event of an accident. In fact, most state laws require auto insurance and as a result insurance companies offer competitive rates. Fire insurance, to cover the loss of our homes, is another type of insurance that most of us are familiar with because lending institutions usually require it when they grant a mortgage. The area of insurance that generally poses the greatest problem to women is life insurance.

Life Insurance

It seems as though there is something sinister about talking about life insurance with your husband. Husbands are apt to remark, "I'm worth more dead than alive," or "I don't want to make *my* wife a wealthy widow." With these types of remarks emerging, it's no wonder that a wife is hesitant to investigate her husband's life insurance policy. Thank goodness, women are now being encouraged to compare rates and find out what types of life insurance are available. A wife is the one who will suffer if the protection is inadequate, so she must determine what her needs are, based on her budget and her ability to earn an income. Busy husbands rarely have time to explore the different types of life insurance available. In some instances they simply buy their life insurance from a friend in the business. Joe, the insurance friend, calls one evening to say that he's in the neighborhood and would like to stop by to explain the latest insurance policies available from his company. The two men sit in the living room discussing Mary Jo's future needs (usually unrealistically) while she keeps herself busy with other things, staying as far away from the conversation as possible. This is a ridiculous situation! Women have to know about and participate in their husband's life insurance decisions.

Most women are the beneficiaries of life insurance policies purchased by their husbands. The main reason we have life insurance is to replace our husband's income when he dies. It is our protection against the loss of his support. This protection is especially important for the young couple because it probably represents one of their few assets. Most young couples owe more than they own and if the husband dies, the death benefit from his life insurance policy may be the primary source of income for his wife. It is vital that you know how much insurance you might need.

Until recently, life insurance purchasing has been considered a man's responsibility. I feel that a wife should know all she can about her husband's life insurance policy because she is the one who will be most affected if the coverage is inadequate. There are many different kinds of life insurance, but only rarely does the insurance agent inform a prospective client of the choices available.

Life insurance is not an easy product to sell and most insurance agents work on a straight commission basis. Because of this situation, life insurance companies are constantly creating new types of policies as selling incentives for their agents. Commission payments can be greatly increased if a new insurance idea is sold. One of the major life insurance companies lists forty-nine different life insurance policies and prices offering the *same* death benefit. This presents a terrible dilemma for the husband who wants to protect his family the best way he can. In most instances he is presented with only one type of policy to consider and often it is the latest policy the insurance company is trying to sell. I believe that wives should be the ones to purchase life insurance on their husbands. They should ask themselves several questions: What if my husband doesn't come home tonight? What will I have to live on and for how long? How is life insurance priced? What are my choices?

The price of life insurance is based on the number of people of a certain age who can be expected to die within a year's time. Insurance agents have standard mortality tables that show the incidence of death at different ages. The older a person is, the greater the risk of death. The basic cost of life insurance is determined by these figures. It is logical that the cost of insurance will increase as a person gets older. How is it possible then for an insurance agent to claim that if you buy life insurance while you are young the cost will be cheaper and your premium will not increase as you get older? This is a method that insurance companies use to pull the wool over your eyes.

There are two basic types of life insurance: term insurance and cash-valued insurance. Term insurance offers death protection and nothing more. If you die, the insurance company pays the beneficiary the total amount of the policy you purchased. There are no savings involved. You are not building any cash reserves. As long as you pay the premiums you are protected. If you stop paying the premiums (cancel the insurance), you do not get any money back. If bought with care after studying your income needs, term insurance is the cheapest life insurance you can buy that will give you adequate protection against your husband's death. The word "term" is a bit misleading because you can purchase this type of protection for an indefinite period of time up to age 99. There are many types of term policies available and they can be purchased for almost any time limit you desire (five, ten, twenty years, etc.). The yearly premium increases accordingly as you get older.

Cash-valued insurance is a combination of term insurance and a forced savings account. This is the type of insurance most people own. It serves a dual purpose: to provide a death benefit and to build a nest egg for the future. As the nest egg increases, the risk to the insurance company decreases, so the increased cost due to aging doesn't show. Cash-valued policies are known by many names. Several common ones are Whole Life, Ordinary Life, 20-Pay Life, 30-Pay Life, and Endowments. The prices of these policies are based on the cost of term insurance, plus the amount of savings included in the policy. Do you receive the death benefit and the amount of your savings at death? The answer is no. You only receive the death benefit. What happened to the savings account? It is returned to you as part of the death benefit. In fact, some companies acknowledge that in time you eliminate the entire risk to the insurance company and therefore they will pay you the total death benefit when you reach 90. Why haven't you been told about this? It's all been kept very secret.

I became aware of this life insurance game back in 1957 when I began to reconsider some of the rules I was following in family financial planning. Since I grew up during the Depression, the word SECURITY was etched on my soul. When Cam and I first started our family financial plan we wanted to get things paid for as quickly as possible. We thought it was the only way we could protect ourselves against the next depression. So, we had a twenty-year plan— pay for our house in twenty years, pay for our insurance in twenty years, etc. We thought if we worked hard enough we could be secure in our old age . . . ha, ha. Then I discovered that the devil I should have been guarding against was not a depression but inflation—a word that was totally new to me and most of us at that time. The dollars I had been salting away in our 20-Pay Life policy would be worth so much less by the time I needed them that I would have to increase the value of the policy continually in order to obtain a realistic death benefit. I looked at all of the cash-valued insurance we owned, saw the accumulated cash, and realized that we were paying an extraordinary amount of money for a meager death benefit. I also realized that the money sitting in our cash-valued policy wasn't working for us.

So I decided to go shopping for term insurance. I still wanted death benefit protection, but I didn't want our savings sitting in an insurance policy. I wanted that money to be someplace where it would be earning interest. I was amazed to find that no one would sell me a term insurance policy. I could only buy term insurance if I purchased another cash-valued policy and added some term insurance onto that policy as a rider. Well, to make a long story short, I dumped the policy I had even though I wasn't able to replace it with term insurance. I was taking a great risk, but Cam said the decision was mine because the reason we had a life insurance policy was to protect me when he died. I was the one who would have to assume the risk and respon-sibility, and I did. I went back to work so that if anything happened to Cam I would be able to support John and myself. I am happy to say that you won't have to go through this. There are now many insurance companies that will sell pure death protection (term insurance) at reasonable rates.

I think this is great news, because I've found that most wives are underprotected against the loss of their husband's income. The cost of cash-valued insurance can be as much as 400 to 500 per cent greater than term insurance because of the forced savings factor. When a young couple is first starting out with a new home and small children they can rarely afford a savings program, as wise as it may be. When they are sold a cash-valued policy, they can only afford a small amount of protection in that package. I feel that the cash-valued life insurance policy is a luxury few young couples can afford. If you can afford an adequate death benefit and a savings account, be my guest, but in all the years I've been talking to women about finances I've found that most of them don't have a realistic amount of death protection because they think they can't afford it. Now, with the arrival of insurance companies that specialize in term life insurance women can afford to get the protection they need. I think every young mother should have enough death protection to replace her husband's income for several years so that she can have the choice of staying at home or work-ing, especially during her children's "little years."

Inadequate protection can result in tragedy for the young widow with children. Take, for example, the story of two young families I knew several years ago. They both lived in one of those new, closely knit neighborhoods with couples in their thirties, small children, and husbands who were at the beginning of their careers. One Sunday, two of these young husbands were killed in a car accident on their way home from the golf course. Instantly, the neighborhood rallied to help the two young widows and their children. After the funerals the neighbors were naturally curious and concerned about the finances of both these young gals.

As it turned out, John's wife received $100,000 from his life insurance policy. She would be able to stay in their new house and her children would not have to be uprooted from their friends and school. In short, her future was secure for a number of years. Mark's wife was not as fortunate. His policy only paid her $25,000. She had no choice but to move back in with her parents.

Why did this have to happen? Both Mark and John were the same age; both had taken out life insurance policies soon after they moved into their new homes; and both had bought their policies from the same company, at almost the same cost. The difference was that John's policy was term insurance and Mark's policy was cash-valued insurance with a forced savings feature built into the cost, an advantage, Mark thought, in building a retirement fund. The real difference between the two policies, however, turned out to be $75,000 more for John's widow than for Mark's.

The ups and downs of a family's finances are not predictable. There are times when you can save and there are times when you can't put away a penny. I don't like to see a mandatory amount going into savings because of a contract. When a life insurance policy has a large savings feature involved, it becomes a contract and that premium must be paid or the protection is lost. I can hear the insurance agent's pitch now, telling you how you'll be able to borrow on your cash-valued policy at low, low interest rates and other advantages of a cash-valued policy. I think this is dumb—to set up a situation where you are forced to borrow your own money out of the insurance policy to pay the premiums on that same policy. To add insult to injury, you have to pay a higher interest on the money you are borrowing (which is *your own* money) than the insurance company pays you on that money that is sitting in the cash-valued portion of your policy. Then, if you fail to repay the loan, it is subtracted from your death benefit. None of this makes any sense to me.

I want a woman to have sufficient death protection so that if her husband dies, she will have time to determine her next move. Today that means a minimum of $100,000. This amount is affordable if you buy term insurance. I think a young family should have long-range goals of accumulating money, but I don't want them to sacrifice death benefit protection to do it. If you can separate life insurance from the savings feature of life insurance, and have the discipline to save elsewhere, your money will do much better in a savings account at a bank or savings and loan institution.

Many people think that life insurance is meant to last forever, and that all women, regardless of age, should have the protection of an insurance policy on their husband's life. I disagree. I feel that a woman should have a $100,000 death benefit in life insurance until she is 45 or 50. I view financial planning as having a goal of accruing $100,000 by the time you reach 65 or retirement age. You can allow the death benefit to decrease as you get closer and closer to reaching that goal of $100,000. As your assets and savings grow, you can cut back on life insurance.

When you think of life insurance as replacing a husband's income if he should die, then you see that the less years of work he has left, the less insurance you need. Also, since the true cost of insurance is based on his age, by the time he is 60 the cost of life insurance will be too expensive for you to afford. And once he retires you are not going to be able to continue to pay large premiums on a limited income. All of these facts reinforce the idea that life insurance is meant to be a temporary expense. You should try to replace the life insurance with money so that by the time you are 60 you own the death benefit in personal assets. If you don't have the assets, in this case $100,000, to replace the death benefit, you are taking a large risk in eliminating that policy. It's a large responsibility, to accumulate sufficient assets to replace life insurance, but well worth it, if you can manage your savings. Large amounts of money should be looked at realistically. I continue to see women in their 60s holding on to their husbands' old life insurance policies as though they really meant something. Many of these policies only have a death benefit of $10,000. It's sad to see, especially since $10,000 doesn't last very long today.

My first meeting with an insurance agent was back in the 1930s, shortly after I landed my first full-time job. My father felt that I should have an insurance policy as a forced savings. (Little did he know how I would turn out.) Anyway, I was *sold* a 20-Pay Life insurance policy with a $2,000 death benefit. The annual premium on that policy was $60, one month's income for me. If I paid $60 a year for twenty years, the policy would be paid for at the end of twenty years. I would have free life insurance ($2,000!) for the rest of my life. Since I was only 20 when I bought the policy, it would be paid for by the time I was 40. I could sit back and wait to die.

There is an important aspect of this life insurance policy that I want to discuss—the cash-value of the policy. By the time I reached 40, I would have paid $1,200 in premiums, exactly the amount of cash value in my policy. I had almost paid the entire amount of my death benefit by this time. Of course, this is a big selling point for this type of policy. It is called *net cost*, and what it means is that you can cancel the policy and receive a check for $1,200, hence your insurance coverage for the past twenty years has cost you nothing. Be careful here. That insurance coverage does cost you something—the lost income you would have received if the money had been earning interest in a savings account. If that $2,000 policy was meant to protect someone against the loss of my income, it was almost worthless. And if the policy had been purchased as a forced savings account, I could have done much better investing it elsewhere.

You can take this argument a step further and examine it from the point of view that at 40 I had a paid-up life insurance policy. There would be no insurance costs for the rest of my life. No cost? If I had that $1,200 in a savings account it would be earning $72 a year at 6 per cent annual interest. That $72 is the actual cost of my insurance. Since I had already paid $1,200 in premiums, I would be paying $72 a year for $800 of protection ($2,000 minus $1,200 = $800). This is an exorbitant price to pay for so little insurance.

When I reached 40 I had two choices as to what I could do with that policy: I could leave it alone and at my death my estate (husband, children) would receive $2,000 or I could cancel the policy and take my $1,200 and invest it elsewhere. I decided to invest my money elsewhere. I put it in a safe investment where it earned a little more than 7 per cent annual interest. By the time I was 50, that money had doubled to $2,400 and by the time I was 60, it had doubled again to $4,800. If I make it to 70, which I'm sure I will, it will double again to $9,600. And if I make it to 80? Well, you see my point. If that money was meant to take care of me in my old age, I certainly made a wise decision in taking it out of the hands of the insurance company. However, if I had taken that $1,200 and spent it, I would have nothing.

There is one thing I want to stress here. If for any reason you decide you want to change the life insurance policy on your husband's life, don't let go of that old policy before you have another policy in your hand—and not before you have read it over thoroughly and discussed it with your insurance agent. You want to make sure that any new policy you buy is adequate.

I don't think that any woman should expect to be supported for the rest of her life. I don't want women to feel *that* well protected. I would like a woman to have adequate funds so that if her husband dies she will have the choice of going back to work or staying home with her children until they no longer require her constant attention. Your first step should be to find a part-time job so that by the time your children leave the nest you will have skills and a job that requires most of your time.

Why do I feel a woman should have a job? Well, I think it is the soundest mental health program I can imagine. You don't have to become a career woman, climbing the corporate ladder. (Unless, of course, that's what you want.) I think a woman should have to get up every morning, put on her girdle (well, I still have to), put a smile on her face, and go forth to face the world. I fear for the woman who has all the money she needs and has no place to go every day. You don't have to make a great deal of money, but you should work for the extra money you need for travel, gifts to the kids, etc.

So, how much life insurance do you really need? Begin by taking a look at your monthly budget. Once you know how much you need to live on a month, multiply it by the twelve months of the year and then multiply that figure by the number of years that you will need to be supported. (See tables at the back of the book.) Next, make a list of your present assets. Find out what benefits you are entitled to from your husband's employer. Then, and this is most important, take a trip to the local Social Security office and find out what benefits you would receive and for how long, in the event of your husband's death. The length of time you are entitled to receive these benefits is essential in your planning. You will not receive any Social Security benefit unless you are the mother of a child under the age of eighteen. Also, find out if you can receive benefits from the State Workmen's Compensation Fund if your husband is killed while at work. Check out all of these things for yourself. Then you will know how much life insurance you need on your husband.

As I mentioned earlier, I feel that the minimum amount of life insurance today should be $100,000. This amount won't support a woman for the rest of her life, but it will give her time to adjust to her new life. Most men will hit the ceiling when you mention a $100,000 policy, even if they are earning $25,000 a year and $100,000 only amounts to four years of their salary. We still haven't realized what inflation has done to our salaries. A policy for $100,000 isn't that great, and it won't make you a wealthy widow. (See tables at the back of the book.)

Who Needs Insurance?

A close friend of mine was married to a very successful plumbing contractor. He owned three trucks and was building quite a business for himself. Tom had a great knack for bidding on a job and making money at it. He was also a family man and was proud of himself because his home was actually *paid for* in full. If anything happened to him, his wife Nancy and their two small children wouldn't have to worry about the mortgage payments. They would be secure.

Also, because Tom was such an energetic and aggressive man, he had also bought some undeveloped land in the San Fernando Valley of California, an exceptionally good idea at the time. Of course, he also had large monthly payments and taxes to pay on his investments, but his contracting business handled that nicely. My concern was what would happen to my friend Nancy if Tom died. She could continue to live in their home, but she would have no money to pay for groceries or the payments on their investment real estate. She might be forced to sell the real estate for less than it was worth because she wouldn't have time to wait for the right offer.

Tom wouldn't even consider getting a life insurance policy. He hated life insurance salesmen and he had only been presented an expensive cash-valued life insurance policy. He didn't even know that term policies existed. If he had taken out a term policy for $50,000, which only would have cost a couple of hundred dollars a year, Nancy would have been assured of a few financially secure years in which to decide what she should do. A small amount of term insurance would have guaranteed Nancy some cash so she could buy groceries and meet the monthly real estate payments. Life insurance does produce instant cash.

Another situation where life insurance should be considered is if your husband is in business with another person (a partnership). What would happen to your husband's business if his partner died? In many instances, his partner's wife would inherit half of the business. If you and your husband didn't have the assets to buy her out, you would have a sticky problem on your hands. The shoe could also be on the other foot. If your husband dies, does his partner have the assets to buy you out? There is an easy solution to this problem. Both partners draw up a buy/sell agreement. This agreement states that the business is worth a certain amount of dollars and if either partner should die, his widow agrees to sell her half at the stated value of the buy/sell agreement. The surviving partner also agrees to buy the business at the agreed price. Where does he get the money to do this? From term insurance. At a minor expense to the partnership, each partner purchases a term policy on the other's life. This gives both partners a choice in determining what they will do with the business if one of the partners dies.

Who Should Own The Life Insurance Policy?

I feel strongly that a wife should not only be the beneficiary of her husband's life insurance policy, but also the owner of the policy. For many years we have had to pay death taxes on almost all estates. If the wife owned the life insurance policy she would not have to pay death taxes on the insurance money because she would be receiving her own property. Therefore, estate planners recommended that the ownership of a husband's life insurance policy be in his wife's name. Then there would be no taxes due at the time of death.

In 1976 the tax laws were changed and now most estates will not be subject to death taxes. Though the argument that a wife own her husband's life insurance policy is not as important as it was in the past, I still feel that a woman should own her husband's policy so that she will be protected in case there is a divorce.

If an ex-husband is providing support for a woman and her children, his income is essential to their financial survival, particularly in the first few years following the divorce. If he dies, that support ends and she could find herself and her children on welfare. A divorced woman should keep her ex-husband's life insurance policy and continue to pay the premiums until she is no longer dependent on his support.

Another reason a woman should own her husband's life insurance policy is to have complete control over her protection. The owner of a life insurance policy can borrow against it (if it is a cash-valued policy), cash it in, change the beneficiary at any time, and do any other number of things with the policy.

Many times a husband will use a life insurance policy for business reasons, using the death benefits as collateral on a business loan (this is known as putting an assignment on the policy). This is often not known or understood by the woman for whose protection the policy was originally purchased. If business insurance is needed, it should be purchased separately. If a husband cannot pass a physical exam to purchase a new policy for business reasons, this is all the more reason why he should not tamper with his wife's protection.

When a wife decides to acquire the ownership of her husband's policy it can sometimes result in marital arguments and complicated financial arrangements, but I think it is well worth the problems you may have to face. In some states, a woman must prove that the money she used to pay for the premiums was her own, not her husband's. This means that her husband may have to give her the money to place in a separate checking account so that the check she writes comes out of her own account and not their joint checking account. This could be a messy situation, but if that is the way it has to be done, do it. Question the insurance company's legal department for information on your state's laws. If your financial support comes from another person, that support should be insured, whether you are married or divorced.

Terms You Should Know

The initials WP stand for *waiver of premium*, which means that if the insured person is disabled for six months or more, the premium will be paid by the insurance company until that person is well again or death occurs. The cost for this additional coverage is usually pennies and is well worth it.

A *double indemnity* clause can be added to your insurance policy to increase the death benefit in case the insured dies as the result of an accident. The cost of this additional coverage is usually around $1.50 per $1000 of coverage. It is an inexpensive way of increasing your death benefit, but should not be added if it would lower the original coverage for death from a cause other than accident.

How Should You Pay Your Insurance Premiums?

Most insurance companies offer you the option of paying for your premiums on an annual, quarterly, or monthly basis. If you pay on an annual basis, you are making an advance payment for a year's worth of coverage. But, if you pay on a quarterly or monthly basis, there is usually an additional interest charge of 9 per cent on the cost of the annual premium. This interest charge is seldom discussed when you purchase insurance. The best way to avoid paying this interest charge or having to pay for coverage in advance is to work out an arrangement with your bank for an automatic monthly withdrawal that is paid directly to the insurance company. Most insurance companies will agree to this arrangement. They can eliminate the cost of billing you and they can also avoid late payments. The insurance company simply asks the policy owner to sign a bank withdrawal authorization slip, which allows the insurance company to draw a check from your account on a fixed date every month. This may seem like a bother, but it is well worth it to avoid paying an interest charge. Also, it allows you to make better use of your money by paying for the insurance premium a month at a time rather than paying for the premium in one lump sum in advance. The one thing you have to remember is to make sure there is enough money in your checking account when the insurance company draws its check.

Life Insurance Traps

There are many different ways that life insurance is sold and one method that is used to entice people with high incomes is by claiming that the policy presents a tax advantage. *Minimum Deposit* is a method of selling a cash-valued policy to people whose incomes fall in a high tax bracket. First, the insurance agent proves that the customer needs a cash-valued policy in excess of $100,000. The premiums are very expensive, but the agent says he can reduce the cost very easily. After contributing to the policy for four years, Mr. Jones can begin to borrow some of the cash values in his policy to help pay the high premiums. Also, since Mr. Jones is in such a high tax bracket, the interest he is charged for borrowing the money is really one half the actual amount, because it is *tax deductible*.

This is what I call a snow job. Mr. Jones is far too busy with his own profession to investigate the policy thoroughly, so he signs. The biggest problem with this situation is that as the years go by, the interest is going to mount up, and the loan against the policy (which you pay back at death) gets larger. What do you do to get out of this mess? You search frantically for another policy, but you can't pass a physical, so you are locked into this pattern because your family needs the protection. I don't believe in borrowing money from your policy, even if the interest rates are low. If you originally purchased a policy because of its forced savings aspect, then you are defeating your purpose. Don't get involved in this supposedly fantastic "tax saver."

There is one rule of thumb that applies to all financial transactions: keep it simple. If the transaction becomes so entangled that you don't understand what is going on, stop the transaction and take a good hard look at the whole situation because you are probably being taken for a ride. The commissions on the sale of Minimum Deposit life insurance can be very lucrative. Just remember that you can't get something for nothing and somewhere in that transaction, probably buried deep in the technical jargon of the policy, there is a substantial cost to you, the customer.

Another thing I'd like to warn you about is mail-order insurance. Never, but never, buy insurance through the mail. It is so costly that you wouldn't believe it. The most prevalent type of mail order insurance is aimed at the elderly who fall prey to these types of policies.

Let's take a look at the case of dear Aunt Maude. She is 70 and has never had much money. She knows she is not going to live forever (she may be surprised) and she would love to leave some money to her favorite niece. As a member of a respected senior citizen organization she receives their monthly bulletin, which often advertises "inexpensive" life insurance policies. She decides to purchase a $2,500 life insurance policy that only costs a few dollars a month.

Poor Aunt Maude! She didn't read the fine print in the policy that states that she must own the policy for at least three years in order to get the $2,500 death benefit. Now she is also out of pocket a few dollars a month that she needs to live on. Stay away from all mail order insurance. Buy your insurance from a reputable insurance company, with an agent you can talk to and ask hard questions.

These are only two examples of the possible pitfalls of life insurance that everyone should be aware of. It's important to investigate any policy thoroughly before you buy it. This also holds true for the policy you currently own. Make sure you are putting your money to the best possible use.

What if you discover that you own a policy that is bleeding you dry? What do you do? You probably figure that you've already poured so much into it that you'll take a great loss if you pull out. I believe that if you own something that you don't want or that is bleeding you dry of needed income, you should get rid of it. Why keep compounding the situation? Cash it in, get what you can out of it, and forget your losses. Buy something that is right for you and your family. Why hang on to a bad investment? Ask yourself this question, "Would I buy this today?" If the answer is no, get rid of it. Again, before you cancel your current policy, make sure you have a replacement in your possession.

Other Types of Life Insurance

When you borrow money to buy a home you are sometimes required to purchase *mortgage insurance* on your loan. This is just another form of life insurance so you should investigate the rates offered by insurance companies that sell term insurance. Often, the lending agent will send you a policy and ask that you sign. Most of the time the policy is more expensive than one you could find on your own. Find out what kinds of term insurance are available. You will be looking at 30-Year Reducing Term policies, in which the death benefit decreases at the same rate as your mortgage.

I also feel that the beneficiary of this policy should be the wife, not the lending institution. She should be able to decide if it is to her advantage to continue paying off the mortgage on a monthly basis (if her interest rate is low) or pay it all off with the insurance money. The death benefit doesn't automatically pay off the mortgage. Many husbands will argue against this because they feel that if their wives received the insurance money they would spend it all and then the house would have to be sold. This is nonsense!

There is also life insurance offered by credit card companies and credit unions to insure that your debts are paid off if you die. These policies should be examined in the same way as mortgage insurance. Check the rates they offer against what a term policy would cost if you bought it on your own. These rates, offered by credit companies, are not always the cheapest.

The type of insurance offered by these lending institutions is group life insurance. The one instance in which it might be advantageous to purchase this type of insurance is if your husband is in poor health and can't pass a physical examination. It may be the only type of insurance you can get.

Annuities

The main attraction of annuities is that they offer a guaranteed lifetime income. They provide security for an elderly person who fears that she may have nothing to live on in her later years. The disadvantage of an annuity is that it is a low income producing investment.

Insurance companies have merchandised this type of investment for many years. They use statistics (standard mortality tables) to determine the average life expectancy for people of different ages and figure out how many monthly checks they will have to pay. They guarantee a very low interest rate on the money you invest and pay you a monthly income. What they actually do is give you back some of your money with a small amount of interest added. Most people who sign up for annuities don't realize that they are consuming their own money. Insurance companies also expect to receive a greater return from investing your money than the interest they pay you. If you die early, the insurance company wins, but if you live to a ripe old age, you've made a sound investment. Many of us are sure that we will outlive the national averages and therefore we sign up for annuities. Be aware of what this type of investment actually entails.

If an annuity will bring you peace of mind then the low earnings aren't such a drawback. But, whatever you decide to do, don't place the greater portion of your total assets in an annuity or any type of investment where you receive a fixed number of dollars every month that cannot be changed in case of an emergency. Some assets should always be placed in a savings account to allow for flexibility.

There are many changes taking place in the life i̶... industry today as a result of growing consu̶... People are no longer blindly buying cash-val̶... way they did in the past. The future trend is̶... inexpensive term policies. Many companies̶... valued policies are concerned about their f̶... good news for consumers. The important th̶... ber about life insurance is that it is not co̶... only insurance companies and their agents̶... appear complicated.

Homeowner's Insurance

Our homes are probably the most valuab̶... we own so we must make sure they are adequat̶... Originally, homeowner's insurance only offer̶... against the loss of your home because of fire,̶... surance companies market a homeowner's "p̶... includes insurance against theft, vandalism, f̶... damage, and public liability. Coverage for̶... floods, and other natural disasters is availabl̶... parts of the country. Only you can decide wh̶... likely causes of damage would be for your home.

These packages are often an inexpensive way to buy comprehensive insurance on your home because they include large amounts of public liability. This type of insurance will protect you against being sued if someone is injured on your property. My homeowner's insurance policy includes coverage for theft and vandalism, which I don't really need, because I live in a safe neighborhood, but it is still cheaper for me to buy a homeowner's package than to pay, on a separate basis, for the different types of insurance I need.

When you buy homeowner's insurance it is important to know the "real" cost of replacing your home. Find out exactly what it would cost to rebuild your home at today's prices before you purchase any insurance. The cost of labor and materials has skyrocketed in the past few years, and prices continue to escalate every year. Make sure your policy is updated periodically to keep up with rising costs.

Homeowner's insurance is usually contracted for three years. Normally, a responsible agent will let you know if you should increase your coverage during that period, but ultimately, you are responsible for checking on this yourself. Remember that in this case the agent is not trying to increase his commission, he's trying to protect your home.

I've updated my policy three times in the past three years. Three years ago the cost of rebuilding my home was $35 per square foot and now it is up to $50 per square foot. By next year, it will probably go up to $60 per square foot.

What about the furnishings and other possessions inside your home? You must keep in mind that your insurance policy won't cover the actual value of all your possessions. Insurance companies will depreciate the value of your possessions according to the length of time you have owned them. "Lady, I'm sure that sofa cost you $600, but, my goodness, you've had it for ten years! I'm sorry, but we can only allow you to claim $180 on it." Try to buy a new sofa for $180!

It is also important to remember the amount of the deductible on your homeowner's policy. I once had a table that someone burned by accident and when I sent in my claim I found out that the insurance company would only reimburse me for the damage that was over $100. It is necessary to prove the value of your household possessions and that they actually exist. You should have an inventory —a written description and photograph—of everything in your home. Have the insurance agent come over and appraise your valuables, so that if you own something that is especially valuable, such as original art, the insurance company is aware of it. (People who rent can purchase Renter's Insurance to protect the furnishings and other personal belongings in their homes.)

Automobile Insurance

The main reason for buying automobile insurance is to protect ourselves against public liability and property damage. If you have an accident and smash into another car, you need to be insured so that you won't be sued. Unfortunately, what has happened in recent years is that the courts have awarded enormous sums to people injured in car accidents and as a result, the cost of adequate insurance coverage has become exorbitant.

As far as I'm concerned, the more coverage you have, the better off you will be. You may think you can't afford to pay the premiums, but there are ways to bring that cost down. For example, you can assume the risk for incidental damages, such as the cost of repairing a fender, by having a large deductible in your policy. If you take that risk and buy a policy with a large deductible of $250, you can lower the cost of your premiums substantially. This doesn't do you much good, however, unless you make a point to have that $250 set aside in a savings account so you can use it if you need to repair your car. Otherwise, you may find yourself in a situation where you don't have the cash available to get the repairs made. Car repair costs have increased faster in the past few years than the cost of buying a new car.

You can also keep the cost of auto insurance down by eliminating the collision insurance on your car. The collision insurance pays for the cost of repairing or replacing your car if you damage it. If you own a beat-up 1957 Chevy, the annual cost of collision insurance is probably higher than the cost of replacing your car, so you don't need collision insurance. On the other hand, if you own a new car you need to have collision insurance.

When your children start to drive, you will find that the cost of your insurance premiums will probably triple in cost. Insurance companies consider anyone under the age of 25 a high risk driver. They have statistics to prove that young drivers are careless and irresponsible. If you own the car that your child drives, you should make sure that you are adequately covered.

Health Insurance

The rising cost of health care has made front page news for the past several years. There is no getting around it—health care costs are outrageously expensive. Because of this fact, it is difficult on an average income to obtain complete insurance coverage for all the medical expenses you might encounter. The cost of health care has become one of the major concerns of the nation and the Congress has been discussing for some time the possibility of national health insurance. Another health care program that has been gaining in popularity is Health Maintenance Organizations (HMOs). The best known of the HMOs is probably the Kaiser Medical Plan, which originated in California during World War II. HMOs are clinics that offer all medical services under one roof. You pay a set fee to participate in the plan, where the primary focus is on preventive medicine. The only drawback to these HMOs, many people feel, is that you have little control over the selection of doctors or facilities. HMOs are continuing to gain in popularity, however, and many large corporations are even looking into the possibility of setting up their own HMOs for their employees. These new health facilities represent a growing trend, and might possibly solve the problem of today's exorbitant medical costs.

The first thing you should know about health insurance is that the average hospital stay for a person under 65 is seven days. According to the latest statistics, the cost for one day in the hospital is $165, not including surgical fees, special care, medication, and other expenses. If your insurance only pays you $50 a day, you are inadequately covered. Be sure to check the surgical schedule provided by your insurance company. If it says that they will pay you $250 for an appendectomy and the going rate is $750, you are not covered. Also, find out how soon your insurance coverage takes effect. If coverage doesn't start until after the eighth day in the hospital you've got problems because you will probably be home by then. Read the policy! Do not assume that you are covered for anything. Major medical expenses can wipe out your family savings and also create enormous additional debts.

All medical insurance is expensive, but you can bring the cost down by assuming responsibility for the day-to-day expenses, such as going to the doctor for a flu shot. You assume this risk by having a large deductible on your policy. The larger the deductible, the cheaper the premium. Again, as with automobile insurance, you must be sure to set aside the deductible amount. It may seem like a lot of money to set aside, but if you put it in a savings account, you can collect interest on it. Also, the amount that you will save in premiums will far exceed the amount of the deductible that you set aside.

Watch out for exemptions listed in your policy. If you have had a medical problem in the past and change policies, your new policy may list an exemption that will not cover you if that old medical problem reoccurs.

These are just suggestions, but I think it is important to be aware of alternate ways of doing things. Just because everyone is hollering that you *must* have medical insurance for everything, including hangnails, doesn't mean that it is true. You have to decide which type of medical insurance best suits your needs, so examine all the options that are available.

One last note on health insurance. Many elderly people have the mistaken idea that they can make money from health insurance. There is a disease that sets in with old age and that is that some people become misers. Possibly because their lives often become ingrown, they not only become stingy and suspicious, but they start to believe that they can be very crafty and make a bundle from *health insurance!* All too often insurance agents are aware of this and continue to sell these policies. Every day old people are taking out new health insurance policies on which they will never be able to collect. Some people have as many as four or five different policies. Whenever possible, the elderly should have another responsible party be the judge of the adequacy of their current protection. The buying of policy upon policy should be discouraged; there is no way to "make money" from any kind of insurance.

The insurance industry in this country is an enormous money-making business. For some reason insurance has been made to appear too complex for the average citizen to understand. This is not true. It does seem confusing at times, but with a little perseverance on your part I don't think you will have too much trouble finding the right insurance to fit your needs. The insurance industry is in a state of flux, however, so you have to be alert to the changes that are taking place. In the next few years there will be new insurance products that will be offered as the competition for your dollars continues to grow. Many states are considering the advantages of no-fault car insurance and professionals in the health care system are continually examining ways to provide better and cheaper health care. Be aware of these changes because they can have a great impact on you and your family. Someone, and I hope that it is you, must stay on top of the situation.

DON'T WORRY DEAR, IT'S A GOOD INVESTMENT.

L&G BOMB LEONES
EMPORIUM
CHEAP GOODS
*WRIST WATCHES
*CAMERAS
*GOLD MINE STOCK
★ ★ ★ ★
TODAY'S SPECIAL
BROOKLYN
BRIDGE
INVEST TODAY!!!

Chapter Four   # Investments

We've talked a great deal about ways of careful money management that can make it possible for your family to save money. Now we're going to look at all the different options you can choose to make those savings grow. It's a challenge and there are risks, but the benefits can be fantastic.

Few of us can manage to save large sums of money from our monthly income. Most of our income is needed for the day-to-day expenses of living. The trick is to take whatever money we are able to set aside and put it someplace where it can grow. There is usually a certain amount of risk involved no matter where you put your money. This element of risk is one area where women are apt to be too cautious. Most women have a kind of cookie-jar philosophy of money. The only money that has any reality is the $20 we manage to save every month. We have not been programmed to take risks. We have been taught to be cautious and as a result we are reluctant to take risks, not only with money, but in many other facets of our lives. I'm not saying that being cautious is wrong, it's only wrong when it makes you too timid or inflexible to take a chance on something that could bring you happiness in the long run.

You can change; I did. When I was a young bride and Cam was off at war, I was living in Los Angeles and Cam wrote me and said that he wanted me to buy some property because all the guys in his outfit and a lot of others were talking about moving to Los Angeles after the war. Well, I couldn't do it! The very idea scared me to death! Gosh, if I could turn back the clock what a killing I'd make today! But as the cliché goes, "live and learn."

Taking risks with your money can give you butterflies at first, but as you become more self-confident, you may find it a challenge. Now I'm not saying you should run out and throw all of your savings into some high risk, speculative venture; all I'm saying is don't back away from something just because there is an element of risk. There is no "safe" investment for any of us, but there are different degrees of risks you can take.

When you are young you can afford to take chances, because if you make a mistake and lose some money you have enough years ahead of you to replace it. The classic formula for investing money is to put one-third of your total in a savings investment and guaranteed savings accounts, eliminating as much risk as possible; one-third in an investment that has potential growth, and hence slightly more risk; and one-third in a speculative investment. My idea of speculation is not buying a hundred shares of XYZ stock. I think a speculative financial venture should be personal. It should be something you can be involved in and enjoy. You may not enjoy buying shares of XYZ stock, but you might enjoy investing with someone who is filming a documentary or who is starting out in business with a terrific idea that you believe in, such as a new method of harvesting lobsters. Speculation should be something that's fun and if you don't make it this time, perhaps you will next time.

As you grow older your pattern of investment will have to change. Usually it's wise to start giving up some of the growth potential investments and the speculations, because the older you get, the less years you have to recoup your losses. This is particularly true as you approach retirement age. Then you will start using the money that you've been investing over the years. You start eating the eggs, and in time even some of the chickens.

The one-third breakdown formula will not suit everyone's financial situation. There are other factors that need to be considered when deciding to invest your savings. Do you need additional monthly income? What portion of your assets are needed to produce this additional income? Do you have an income tax problem? How much money can you afford to have in a no-income (potential growth) investment? If you need cash for emergencies, can you get it quickly? The answers to these questions should help you decide where to invest your money.

Every investment you make should serve a specific purpose. You must understand how it works and what it is doing for you, otherwise you are not in control and in the long run you may be the loser. You could also end up feeling as silly as I did after my first venture into the stock market.

One year Cam and I sold some property and suddenly found ourselves with a nice little chunk of money that we wanted to invest. After listening to all our neighborhood financial geniuses and Cam's friends from work, we wanted to buy. Oh, we had a great time! We bought twelves shares of one stock, fourteen of another and so on. About a month later we received our stock certificates, which were so colorful and exciting to have in our hot little hands. We also received a few dividend checks that we quickly spent. Boy, were we in the BIG TIME! We soon discovered, however, that some of our stocks didn't pay dividends. Well, that was no fun so we sold those. And so it went. What a mess! We didn't know what we were doing, what we had bought, or what we were supposed to do with our stocks. The bloom began to fade from our great adventure as we became more and more confused.

This is when I started to learn about investments. I realized that we had to know what we owned, why we wanted to own it, when we should sell, and so forth. Fortunately, the whole affair turned out to be a cheap lesson. I want you to be able to avoid these unnecessary pitfalls.

In actuality there are only a couple of things that you can do with your money. You can loan your money or you can buy something with it. It sounds simple, but what do these two options really mean?

Loaning

There are many places you can loan money, and what really occurs is that you are renting your money (for a specified time period) for someone else's use. That someone promises that they will pay you back not only the amount you have loaned, but also an additional amount (interest) for the use of your money. How much interest you get depends on several factors: how much you loaned; how long you loaned it for; and who you loaned it to. When you buy something you are basically saying, "I think this item will be worth more at a future date and then I will sell it and make a profit."

The most obvious place to loan money is to a bank, although most of us don't realize it. Your savings account at the local bank or savings and loan association is a loan. You put your money in a savings account and the bank pays you interest on your money. As soon as it goes in they turn around and loan it right back out to the person who wants to buy a house, car, etc. And this person in turn pays back the loan each month and these payments are put back in the pot and loaned out again. Normally, your money will be used nine times a year by the bank. This is how they make money. They pay you interest on your savings account, but charge much higher interest rates on the money they loan.

By the way, are you sure that your bank provides the maximum return possible on your savings account? Before you open a savings account you should shop around carefully. The bank at the corner may be convenient, but does it give you the best return on your money? Many banks and savings and loan associations require a minimum deposit before they pay interest and some even require that your money must remain in the account for a certain length of time before they will begin to pay you interest. Check it out. Did you know, for instance, that by Federal law, savings and loan associations are allowed to pay ¼ per cent more interest than banks? They are also allowed to offer such extra benefits as free safe deposit boxes and traveler's checks. Shop around and get the most out of your investment.

You're probably wondering what possible risk could be involved in opening a savings account. Even though most banks and savings and loan associations are members of the Federal Depositor's Insurance Corporation (FDIC), there is a small risk to the investor. Your bank's membership in this insurance company only protects you against the mismanagement of funds. Member banks pay premiums into the FDIC and if someone makes off with bank funds or the bank makes poor investments, the insurance company steps in and stops all transactions and slowly pays off the depositors. It doesn't happen often, so don't worry about it, but it is something you should be aware of. You are not guaranteed against a depression. There isn't enough money available to pay off all the deposits in banks and savings and loan associations in the U.S. Don't panic though, the system works.

A standard passbook savings account is a good place to put some of your money. It's earning interest; you can take it out any time you need it; and there is practically no risk involved. It's the money you need to have available for emergencies and those once-a-year expenses we spoke about in Chapter 2 (Money Management). Banks and savings and loan associations also have long-term savings accounts called Certificates of Deposit, which require you to keep your money in an account for several years. They can pay you a higher interest rate, but you must leave it in the account for the specified time period or you will have to pay a penalty for early withdrawal.

Another place that you can set up a savings account is through a company credit union. They usually pay excellent interest rates and can offer you an easy savings program called an automatic savings plan. Before you get your paycheck, a certain amount (which you have decided upon) is taken out and put in your savings account before you ever get the check. (Some banks also offer this service.)

Perhaps the safest loan is to the U.S. Government. There is very little risk involved because the government has the ability to tax its citizens to get money to pay you back. The government borrows money for varying lengths of time and the interest rates it pays fluctuate according to the demand for money at the time of the borrowing. If corporations, individuals, banks, and government agencies are trying to borrow money at the same time, the interest rate will be higher than when the demand is less.

Most of us are familiar with government E Bonds, which are more commonly known as savings bonds. You buy a bond for $18.75, hold it for a number of years, and then cash it in for the face value of $25.00. The interest on this bond is the $6.25 you receive when you cash the bond. You don't have to pay tax on this interest until the time that you cash it in. These bonds have been popular since the days of World War II and many people have ended up with stacks of matured (ready to be cashed in) bonds. The problem is that you will have to pay taxes on the interest when you cash them in and if you have a lot of them it could become expensive. What can you do about it? First find out how much tax is involved before you decide you need to save taxes. Sometimes paying the taxes due may be cheaper than trying to lessen the tax or avoid paying it.

If you find that you need to postpone paying taxes on the accumulated interest from E Bonds you can transfer them over into government H Bonds. An H bond pays interest twice a year so you receive an income based on the full $25.00 H Bond and you only pay taxes in a given year on that income, not on the accumulated E Bond interest. You simply postpone paying those taxes. When the H Bond reaches maturity or is liquidated, your taxes will be based on the accumulated interest from the old E Bond. It's an option worth investigating. If you want to find out more about government bonds contact a Federal Reserve Bank, your own bank, or a brokerage house. They can tell you what is available and what the current interest rates are on different types of government borrowing.

Another type of government-related borrowing program is municipal bonds. These bonds are issued by a water district, power district, sewer district, or any other state or local government agency that is authorized by its voters to issue bonds. The Federal Government wanted to make it easy for these agencies to borrow money without having to pay high interest rates, so the interest on these bonds is exempt from Federal income tax. You may have to pay some state income tax, however, depending on the amount of interest you receive.

Municipal bonds can be purchased for different lengths of time, but generally the longer the term, the greater the interest rate you are paid. The interest paid will again fluctuate according to the demand for money at the time the agency is borrowing.

Municipal bonds are usually for large sums of money so you need to be sure you can afford to have that money locked up for years. Also, before you get involved with any municipal bonds, you must investigate the quality of the district you are loaning to. Just because the name of the agency sounds good, because it is governmental, does not mean that the agency will be able to pay the interest promised or principal when it is due. You should ask the question, "How will this governmental unit be able to raise the money when it is due?" Some municipals that have been issued are worthless because the agency has no way of obtaining the repayment funds.

For example, not long ago a group of people got together and purchased an island in the delta region of northern California. They had great plans for the development of this island: marinas, vacation homes, etc. The owners had even obtained approval from the state to issue municipal bonds. These bonds paid an interest rate of 9 per cent, which was fantastic because most other bonds in the state were only paying 6 per cent. Many people became greedy and sunk all kinds of money into these high-interest bonds. They should have looked a little closer before investing. The group offering the bonds had no way to pay them back because the development plans never materialized. Today, those bonds are worthless, and some people lost a lot of money. You must investigate. Just because a bond is "municipal" doesn't mean it will be a sound investment.

Your brokerage house subscribes to publications or services whose purpose is to investigate the financial soundness of the different districts and they rate them accordingly. Of course, you would only loan to the districts with the highest ratings. A brokerage house can also tell you what bonds are on the market and what interest rates they pay.

You can also loan money to a corporation in the form of a corporate bond. For example you can loan a large company $10,000 for a period of twenty years and they may pay you a higher interest rate than banks or the U.S.

Treasury. These are high-yield corporate bonds. This type of bond can be particularly beneficial for the divorcee with a settlement; the widow with money to invest; or the retired person, all of whom need a high-yield on their money for income. I don't think corporate bonds are a particularly wise choice for the young employed person. You are simply increasing the income you will have to pay taxes on. What you need is an investment for future growth, not current yield.

Now what about the risk factor? There are research firms such as Standard and Poor's and Moody's Investor Services which investigate corporate bonds, as well as municipal bonds. They judge the investment qualities of these bonds and rate them according to a prescribed set of letter codes. For example, using the Standard and Poor's notation system, an AAA rating (the highest they give) would mean that this is a high-grade bond having little risk. A brokerage house can tell you what corporate bonds are available and how they are rated. Standard and Poor's and Moody's can also be found at your local library.

What happens if you have your money in corporate or government bonds and an emergency arises and you need to get your money back quickly? Well, first of all, a brokerage house would have to find someone to buy your bonds. However, since the interest rates on all these bonds can vary from year to year you could find yourself in a situation where you are holding a bond that you bought some years ago, which is paying you less than today's bonds are paying. Who is going to buy your bond when they can get better interest elsewhere? You have to sell your bond for less than you paid. This is called discounting a bond. Discounting a bond gives you an out, but you take a chance on losing some money. This is why it is so important to be sure that you can afford to lock this money up for a long period of time.

What if the reverse situation occurs? What if you need to get rid of a bond and the interest being paid on it is higher than the current interest rates being offered? You would sell the bond for more than the face value amount of the bond and make a profit. This is called selling your bond at premium.

Another way you can loan your money is with a Trust Deed. A Trust Deed is loaning your money to someone buying real estate. There are First Trust Deeds and Second

Trust Deeds; they are better known as mortgages. With Trust Deeds the collateral for your loan is the house or land the person is buying. If they can't make the payments on the loan you can foreclose and get the house.

Normally, an individual will not become involved in a First Trust Deed because the amounts of money are usually very large and the time element is long-term. Savings and loan associations and banks are usually the holders of First Trust Deeds. It is more likely that the individual will become involved in Second Trust Deeds.

You may end up with a Second Trust Deed in selling a home. If your buyer can only come up with part of the downpayment you may want to assist him or her by accepting an IOU (Second Trust Deed). Second Trust Deeds are often written for five years and the monthly payment to you is usually 1 per cent of the amount borrowed. This low monthly payment is designed to make it possible for someone to buy a home, although it will not pay off the debt in five years. At the end of that time period there is still a balance due. This amount can be paid off in one lump sum, known as a balloon payment, or you may end up accepting continued monthly payments. The question you need to ask yourself before you get involved in a Second Trust Deed is how long can you afford to have your money tied up?

First and Second Trust Deeds are often amortized (the total amount is paid off in installment payments), so it is important to know what you own and how it works. A woman I knew sold her home and loaned all of the money from the sale, taking a First Trust Deed. For many years she enjoyed spending the monthly check she received. We met when she only had five years of payments remaining and she started telling me about where she was going to reinvest her principal when the loan was paid off. It's hard to believe, but this woman hadn't realized that the monthly checks she had been getting included the repayment of the principal. When the last payment was made, the loan would be paid off. She thought the checks had only been interest! Know what you own and how it works.

Many people consider loaning money on Second Trust Deeds as a very lucrative investment and this lending can be done through a mortgage broker. The mortgage broker is supposed to research the value of the property and the credit rating of the prospective buyer. The charge for these labors is a portion of the interest paid to you by the borrower. You still get a healthy return on your money, but you also assume all of the risk (it's not the broker's money being lent).

I don't recommend Second Trust Deeds. They are very risky unless you can afford to have large amounts of money in speculative and risky ventures, or unless you are willing to take the time to learn all the ins and outs of a transaction of this nature. You are taking the place of a bank so you have to be as professional as they are.

Another type of loan that people get involved in, is loaning money to people to start businesses. This is fine if you know what you're doing and the risks involved. Most people don't.

My friend Dave came to see me one day about a DEAL he was thinking about getting involved with, one he was terribly excited about. He had met a butcher who had recently moved into the area and was looking for a partner with whom to open a shop. Dave was the prospective partner! The butcher needed $5,000 to start—buying a lease, cabinets, fixtures and, of course, meat. He even had a good location picked out. The butcher would pay Dave 10 per cent interest on his loan until the $5,000 was paid off and after that he would give him a monthly fee. It sounded a bit too good to be true. Rarely does anyone pay a fee once a loan has been paid off. Convincing Dave of this was not easy.

According to Dave there was no risk. He had talked to an attorney who had told him that what they had to do was incorporate and that way Dave couldn't lose any money. Only the corporation could lose money. How nice, but wishful thinking. Dave would write out a check for $5,000 to the butcher, who would spend it on putting the business together. If the endeavor didn't pay off, Dave would lose his $5,000. It was as simple as that. The money would be spent—it would be gone—and until a profit was made there was no way that payments could be made on the loan or the monthly fee. Incorporating didn't mean a thing; it was just a piece of paper. It could not guarantee any profits. Well, you could sue. This is ridiculous. You can't get blood out of a turnip. When the money is spent, it is gone—period. Papers, such as incorporation papers, are only as good as the people who sign them. Remember that.

When you know what you are doing, loaning your money can be an excellent way to achieve your financial goals. In most cases the risk you incur and the return you get are both known factors. All the terms of any loan transaction are laid out in advance. The one disadvantage is that since you know what your return will be it is sometimes not as great as it might be if you were willing to take a greater risk with your money. For that reason many people decide to go the profit route. They are willing to give up a known return for an unknown return because the potential for profit is greater. This is the difference between buying for future profit and loaning your money.

Buying

The catch when you buy something is that the increase in value you are hoping for depends on factors beyond your control. Of course, as with loaning money, the risk will vary depending on what you buy. What you can buy for investment purposes boils down to three different categories: real estate, stocks (ownership in a company), and collectibles, such as gold, silver, gems, stamps, art, etc. (Real estate will be discussed in a later chapter.)

There are many different kinds of stock you can buy, each involving varying degrees of risk. The stock market can be very confusing at times, so I think it might be instructive to set up a mock company which will be called the "Mary Rogers Widget Company."

Mary Rogers has a marvelous widget she's invented that she thinks will sell like hot cakes, but she needs money to be able to manufacture and sell her widget. The first thing she is going to do is offer common stock in her company. When you buy her common stock you are giving her money to build her company and you are assuming total risk. She hasn't promised you a thing. You've bought part ownership in her company strictly on the basis of faith in her widget, her ability to manage the company, and her ability to market and sell the widget. It's a high risk, but you've seen production and believe there's a market for the widget.

Now, let's say that you were right and the company starts making a profit. One of two things can happen: The company will either issue dividends to the stockholders or they may, particularly if it's a new and growing company, decide to put the profits back into the company for expansion and improvements.

If the company continues to do well, more people will become interested in the company and will want to buy whatever shares are offered by stockholders. It is the function of a security broker to negotiate an acceptable price between buyer and seller. This is the old story of supply and demand.

If the company becomes very successful and the price of its stock continues to increase, it may initiate a *stock split*. Many people are confused about what a stock split really means. One day I was having lunch with a woman who told me excitedly that she had just doubled her money in the stock market. Doubled her money? Well, that was quite something, so I wondered if she knew something I didn't. I asked her just *how* she had doubled her money. It seems that she owned shares in a company whose stock had been split. She now owned 100 shares in the company instead of 50. I was sorry to shatter her vision of new-found wealth, but she was no better off now than before the stock split. Yes, she did own 100 shares rather than 50, but the value of her stock had not increased, it had remained the same. She now had 100 shares of stock selling at $50 rather than 50 shares selling at $100. She still had $5,000 worth of stock.

The value of a company doesn't increase simply by rearranging shares of its stock. Why do stock splits occur? There is a large psychological factor involved here. The average person is more inclined to buy ten shares of stock at $10 each rather than one share of stock for $100. Therefore if the price of a company's stock becomes too high it may initiate a stock split to reduce the price of a share and make it more attractive to potential buyers. The main reason for a stock split is to broaden the ownership of a company.

There are other stock classifications available to the investor which offer a lower risk than common stock, but because the risk is less the potential for gain is also less. In the stock market, common stock has the highest risk and offers the highest potential profit. Some of these other classifications and preferred stock, cumulative preferred stock, convertible preferred stock, convertible bonds, mutual funds and options.

Preferred stock is bought for income rather than for potential growth. When you buy preferred stock the company promises you two things. First, they promise to pay you a dividend of a fixed amount each year, which is paid before any dividends are paid to common stockholders (but after interest is paid on any outstanding corporate bonds), and second, they promise you that if the company goes out of business you will be paid before the common stockholders (but again after bonds are paid off).

Preferred stocks do not fluctuate much in price and you always know what income you will receive from them, but remember, the company has not "guaranteed" you a dividend, they have only "promised" you one. The company has to make a profit before any dividends are issued.

Cumulative preferred stock is the same as regular preferred, but an extra feature has been added. If a dividend is not issued for one year, it is added to next year's dividend. In other words, you would get no dividend one year, but double dividends the following year. The double dividend would be paid before the common stockholders are paid any dividend at all.

Convertible preferred stock is an option that allows you to convert your preferred stock, within a specified time, for a stated number of shares of common stocks. Obviously, you wouldn't convert to common stocks unless the exchange would be profitable.

Convertible bonds are corporate bonds, which we discussed earlier, but the convertible bond allows you to convert your bonds to common or preferred stock at a later date if you wish. All of these stock classifications were developed to make investing in a company more attractive.

Common stock involves a high risk and you buy it for potential growth. You buy because you think the company will do well and the demand for its common stock will increase. You buy not for current income, but for its potential growth. You realize your profit—or loss—when you sell the stock.

Once you have decided whether you are interested in owning stock for potential growth or income you have arrived at the basic element for deciding what companies you might want to invest in. Seldom will one company offer the best return in both categories. If you are looking for income you would examine those companies that have a long dividend paying record, proven resistance to the ups and downs of the economy, and a good record of increasing dividends. When you are looking for an investment with growth potential the most important thing to look at is current trends. You should be aware of any products or services that seem to be in great demand by the public. For example, several years ago recreational vehicles were in great demand, but there weren't many producers. One of the companies that got in on the ground floor of the boom was Winnebago and some of the people who had the foresight to buy stock in that company did extremely well. It was a high risk, but the potential for growth was also high.

Another thing to examine is the company's earning potential and whether it is steadily increasing. Dividends are paid out of the earnings, but all earnings are not necessarily paid out in dividends. A growth company would probably issue few dividends and those they did issue would likely be small. The earnings would be reinvested in the company for research and expansion.

If the company is new, does it have adequate capital to make a go of it? What does the management look like? Good idea people do not always make the best businessmen.

The key to wise investing in growth-potential stock and income stock is adequate investigation and your constant management. You must be aware and stay aware of not only what your stock is doing, but also how the economy is doing and what the current trends are. Start looking at some of the business journals such as *Business Week*, *Barron's*, and *The Wall Street Journal*. They are great sources of up-to-date information.

Owning an investment means you have to do some conscious management. You must read the material that is sent to you. You must periodically sit in front of your broker or advisor and ask the questions: How are we doing? Show me. What is the status of this company in comparison to others in the same business?

Grandpa Rogers had bought shares in a savings and loan company in the middle 1950s and it had done very well, so that by selling off some of the shares he and his wife were able to take two trips to Europe. Then along came the 1960s and for more years than I care to think about no dividends were paid and absolutely nothing happened to that investment. Grandpa insisted on hanging on to his shares. Would the professional investor allow his money to sit, earning nothing, for years? You know the answer. The professional would move into a new situation that offered either a better potential for growth or a dividend return. He would not sit and allow that money to produce nothing for years.

Mutual funds are investment companies that accept money from many investors and invest the combined monies in usually a wide variety of companies. The two main ingredients of a mutual fund are diversification and professional management. Let's say you have a little money and you want to buy some stock, but you don't have enough money for diversification (to buy into a selection of different companies); you would buy shares in a mutual fund. Combining all of the money of the small investors creates a large enough amount of money to invest in different companies. When you buy shares in a fund you are part owner of the hundreds of companies the fund invests in and those investments are managed by professionals. But it is different than if you had bought stock in the companies yourself. You don't have voting rights and the dividends you receive are those paid by the companies owned in the investment and passed on to you by the mutual fund. If the fund management has made a profit in buying and selling during the year, a capital gain distribution is also issued. These distributions are considered long-term earnings and you can take advantage of reduced tax treatment.

Each fund has an objective. On the front page of the prospectus it is stated that this particular fund must invest in high-grade common stock or in high-yield bonds, or municipal bonds, or in a balanced fund—a third in bonds, a third in preferred stock, and a third in common stock, etc. There are hundreds of funds and finding the one for you can be a little difficult. If you are interested in buying into a mutual fund, a good way to start your research is by looking at a book called The Wiesenberger Financial Services Marketer. It comes out once a year and you should be able to find it in your local library. The performance charts in this publication only tell you what the different funds have done in the past, not what they will do in the future. They can give you an idea of whether a particular fund has a good past performance record—that is all.

One man I knew, who invested in mutual funds, based his selection of funds strictly on these performance charts. Every three months when the new charts came out he would change his investments to all the funds that had done particularly well during that three months, selling the ones that hadn't done quite as well. He was probably the busiest man on the block. He was constantly rearranging his investments strictly on the basis of a short-term performance chart. This is no way to judge a fund or to manage money. By their nature, mutual funds just don't make dramatic jumps in short periods of time. Keep tabs on the charts to make sure that your fund is doing as well as others of its kind, but don't buy and sell mutual funds because a performance chart says one fund did better than another during a short period of time.

Most mutual funds have a brokerage fee and it generally varies from 4 to 8½ per cent of the amount you invest and is included in the price of your shares. Some funds operate as "no-load" funds, which means they do not charge you a brokerage fee when you buy shares of the fund, but as with all funds they do charge you a management fee of usually ½ of 1 percent per year of the value of each share you own. Whether or not a mutual fund charges a brokerage fee should not be the determining factor in selecting a fund. The quality of the investment should be the major concern.

An investment that is very similar to a mutual fund is a unit trust. An investment company puts together a portfolio of bonds, either corporate or municipal, and they issue (sell) units of that total, large investment. This provides the small investor with diversification, but no further management of that unit trust occurs. You will receive interest earned on those bonds and in time you will begin to receive your own money back as the bonds in the unit trust are called in or mature. The difference from a mutual fund is that a unit trust only involves corporate or municipal bonds and no management is provided beyond the initial selection of the bonds in the unit trust.

Another way to invest your money is by buying *options*. You buy a contract that allows you to buy something at a fixed price within a stated time limit. An option allows you to gamble with a small amount of money, on the ups and downs of the price of the stock, or other items the contract allows you to buy. If the price of the item goes up you can purchase it at the price agreed to on the option contract and then sell immediately for a profit. But if the price of the item goes down, there is no advantage in buying, so the money you paid for the option is lost and the option is worthless. This is a simplistic explanation of options. The trading of options and the types of option contracts available are too complicated to explain in detail in this book. Options can be interesting investments if you have time to explore them and manage them.

Another good way to learn about investing without risking large amounts of money is by participating in an investment club. They generally meet about once a month (the more often the better) and what you do is contribute a fixed amount of money to the club and then everyone participates in investing the club's money. These investments should take risks that you wouldn't ordinarily take with your family's money. If run properly, an investment club can be a great education for the novice and you also get to share in any of the profits it makes on its investments.

My experience with women's stock clubs has been mixed. They are easy to organize and it is easy to collect the monthly contribution to be invested, but it is hard to find those few people who are willing to research the stock market and make the necessary investment decisions. The only way you can benefit from a stock club is by becoming involved in the decision-making process. The most successful stock clubs I know have been in offices (working situations) where the participants were all close by and could meet frequently. Most of these women were business oriented and assumed responsibility for the investments made by the stock club.

A margin account allows you to buy stock with borrowed money. You borrow from your broker to buy stock and you pay him interest on the money you borrow. The law says that you must pay a certain percentage of the purchase price with your own money, but you can borrow (leverage) the balance. Buying on margin can allow you to make a greater profit than if you were limited by the number of shares you could buy with your own money. Usually the person involved in buying on margin is constantly buying and selling (trading). Seldom does anyone borrow (buy on margin) for long period of time—only for temporary purchases and sales. The risk is that if the market goes down, you accelerate your losses by using borrowed money.

These are some of the common choices available to you when you decide to invest your money. Before you start delving deeper into these choices, I'd like to introduce you to some of the research tools and investment language that makes investments a little easier to understand.

First of all let's take a look at the stock market averages we're always hearing about. Most of you are familiar with the Dow Jones Industrial average, but how many of you know what it really means? The Dow Jones 30 Industrials is a hypothetical investment in 30 companies whose ups and downs in price are supposed to represent the current trend in the price of stocks. This index is far too restrictive to be a comprehensive measure of the stock market. The Standard and Poor's 500 shows the current prices of stock in 500 companies and is therefore more representative of the market as a whole. These indexes tell you nothing about your individual stock. Both of these averages are based on a fixed number of companies which, ideally, are supposed to represent a cross section of American businesses. They are useful if you remember that they are indicators of what's happening to the market as a whole.

A tool that you can use to determine the price of an individual company's stock is the Price/Earnings Ratio or P/E, which is the way you will often see it written. The P/E is the current price of the stock divided by the company's earnings per share of common stock. If a stock is selling for $20 per share and the estimated earnings per share are $2, the P/E is ten to one, or as a broker would say, the stock is selling at ten times earnings. You could have a P/E of 40 to 1 with the stock selling at 40 times earnings. This suggests that though the earnings are low, the potential of the stock is great. This is the case with many unknown corporations that become successful.

Other tools that you can and should use when you research stock possibilities are, as I mentioned earlier, the business journals, industry resource books, and a company's annual report. You will be surprised at how much you can find out about the stock market, the economy, current trends and even individual companies by reading publications such as *Business Week* and *The Wall Street Journal*. You can buy them from a newsstand or subscribe to them, or vist your local library. The library will also have some industry (stock market) manuals such as Standard and Poor's or Moody's, which will give you a rundown on the financial status of individual American businesses; the Value Line Composite, which tells you how their selection of American businesses have done on the stock market; or, again, the Wiesenberger Financial Services Marketer, that will tell you everything you ever wanted to know about mutual funds. All of these, and many others, will give you the information you need about different companies in which you might be interested. A company's annual report is also a valuable tool. It gives you the financial status of a company; its future plans; and even tells you about the people who run the company.

Well, as we all know, you can read and read, but how do you ever decide? There are ways of narrowing down your choices. Go back to the original question I asked you. Why are you buying stock? Add to that answer all you've learned about the current trends and you'll find that you can automatically eliminate a vast number of the investment possibilities.

You are not alone in this huge financial morass! You can consult a professional. It's a stockbroker's business to know what's going on. Tell the broker your needs and he or she will make suggestions. Notice that I said *suggestions*. Do not let a stockbroker, financial advisor, or money manager make your decisions for you. Investigate those suggestions and see if you like them. Then you can make logical, well-thought-out decisions. When you decide to buy or loan, you should know what you're buying, the reason for buying, and what the investment is supposed to do for you.

Selling

Loaning money is clear cut. Once you have loaned it there is not much else to do, but if you've bought something there's a little more to the story. When and why do you sell? Buying is easy, selling is a little more difficult. The decision to sell is based on the same reasons for buying.

The criteria for when to sell a stock should be made at the time of purchase. For example, you can decide to hold onto a stock as long as the earnings and dividends continue to increase, or until the price of the stock has increased by X per cent. Stick to your predetermined goal. If you need another criterion, ask yourself whether you would buy the stock today at its present selling price and whether it would fulfill your needs today. If the answer is yes, then hold on to the stock or buy more. If the answer is no, then perhaps there is a better place to invest your money.

This brings up another facet of selling stocks. What if the answer is no, you wouldn't buy the stock today. The logical thing to do would be to sell the stock, but many people can't seem to make this decision. They can't handle the loss they would have to take if they sold the stock. They say, "I'll sell this stock as soon as it gets back up to ___." This is crazy! What if it never gets back up there? It could go down even more! The wise investor knows when to take losses. If you wouldn't buy it today, sell it.

Many people make the mistake of hanging on to stock they don't really want when they inherit it from a loved one. They start to associate the stock with Grandpa rather than with the company whose stock it represents. "Oh, I couldn't sell, Grandpa wouldn't want me to." You don't know why Grandpa bought it—he may not have wanted it either, but just got stuck with it. Please! Judge all inheritances on the basis of whether you would buy the investment today if you had money.

No one is infallible when it comes to investing money. It doesn't make sense to beat a dead horse. Turn the page and get on with tomorrow. I recall a woman who wanted me to audit the cost of her husband's boat. It had been bought with another partner and he and her husband envisioned renting the boat and using it as a tax shelter. All of these plans failed to materialize and this woman was angry. What good would it do to write down all the dreadful details? I'm sure that her husband was just as unhappy as she was. It is a waste of time to chew over the mistakes of yesterday.

You will make mistakes when you start making investments, but because you know the risk you're taking, have decided you can afford that risk, and are carefully managing your investments, the mistakes you make will probably not be disastrous. In short, stay on top of the situation and you'll come out ahead in the long run.

Other Investments

There are a few other things we can buy, besides real estate, which will be discussed in the next chapter, and they are items such as gold, silver and gems. I have a theory as to why people buy these items (and it's not just to make money!). Generally these kinds of possessions are bought because of the fear that they are the only things that will always have a value. In other words, if our system of government falls apart with the resulting destruction of our currency, industry, etc., these items will still have value. This may be true, but there are problems involved with owning these items. They are long-term investments, ones that you have to hold for years before you are likely to make a profit; you have to go to a special broker to buy them; you are at the mercy of whoever appraises them (is it really of the quality they say it is?); you have to have them assayed or appraised before you can sell them; and you must have someplace safe to keep them.

I feel there are easier, less-involved ways to make money. Buying these items is a task for the ultrasophisticated speculator or the professional who deals with these items as a business, a gem dealer, for example. Research and an awareness of the problems you may run into are the keys in making any investment. Be sure the people you are dealing with are reputable and experienced.

An exciting way to get involved with commodities, without the problems of actually owning them, is trading in commodities futures. We've already discussed the glamour commodities such as gold and silver, but actually commodities can be as common as soybeans, cotton, and coffee.

Trading in commodities futures is a guessing game about the weather for the next year and whether it will cause a bumper crop or a freeze that would ruin all the oranges in Florida. This is what I call a gamble! The rewards can sometimes be astronomical, but then so can the losses. You purchase a contract to buy when you think there will be a bumper crop and then you wait to see what happens. It's terribly risky, but it might just be your forte.

One last kind of investment I would like to mention is investing in yourself or another member of the family. This could be the most important decision you ever make. It might mean funding your husband's change of jobs.

Have you ever thought about how horrible it would be to go to a job you hated every day and not be able to do anything about it? I'm sure many men and women are in this spot. Wouldn't it be a good idea to make a plan to be self-supporting for a year during that change of careers? Or maybe, you need a nose job. Don't laugh, it could be what you need to get you going. It may not be as expensive as a nose job, maybe just a tuck or two, but if that's what it takes to get you out of the house and on the road, do it. Additional schooling can also be an investment from which you'll reap the benefits long after it's paid for. The choice is yours. How do you want to spend (or invest) your money?

For example, a friend of mine, named Marian, looked like any other 60-year-old woman sipping her tea at a luncheon counter when I met her. She owned and operated a small shoe store and was quite successful. Marian had been widowed ten years earlier and at that time had been forced to find a job. All she could get was a low paying, part-time job selling shoes in a small shop. She didn't make a great deal of money, but she learned a lot—the art of buying merchandise and selling for a profit. When the owner wanted to sell, she was able to negotiate the purchase. That little part-time job had paid off in education and investment. Should you buy a shop? It would be quite risky, but if you are willing to work hard there are profits to be made. If you can show a lending institution that you have had some training or preparation to manage this venture, you might even be able to go into business without having to invest a great deal of your own money. This is an investment in yourself and your abilities. It could be the wisest investment you ever make.

Many people have asked me how to pick a stockbroker or brokerage house. This is a very difficult question to answer. There are hundreds of stockbrokers and many brokerage houses. The only guideline I can give you is to make sure the firm you're dealing with is legitimate and has a good reputation. Another thing I would be concerned about would be how much time the broker spent finding out about me—my needs and my goals. I would want to feel certain that whoever I was dealing with made an effort to understand me and established good lines of communications. You should feel secure and confident in the person's ability. To a large degree the main requirement is that you feel good about the association and feel that the broker has your best interests in mind.

One thing you should know, however, is that there are two different kinds of brokerage houses. There are traditional houses, which offer "research investment advice" and there are discount brokerages houses, which merely handle your buy/sell transaction. The discount brokerage house is cheaper because it has no research facilities and does not make investment recommendations.

This chapter on investments is not intended to make you an authority. It's aim is to introduce you to the investment choices available. It should give you a sound base to work from and the confidence to ask questions. It is one of the first tools in your progression to financial responsibility. As hard as it may be to believe, I think you'll find that finance can be fascinating. Each new process you learn will increase your confidence and, I think, make you eager to learn even more. You'll make mistakes—we all do—but don't dwell on them. Learn from them and go on to the next challenge.

Chapter Five · **Real Estate**

Land equals security is a concept that is entrenched in our American heritage. Our ancestors believed that owning land was synonymous with achieving security and success. In the past, land was the only income producer that people trusted, but in modern times, particularly since the turn of the twentieth century, people have begun to realize that there are other things you can own that also produce security and success. Still, the romantic notion of land ownership is deeply ingrained in all of us.

The treasured dream of the white picket fence and the vine-covered cottage is still with us, and the primary goal for most people in this country is owning their own home. When Cam and I were first married we took many Sunday drives in the country and often we'd see a lush green hill with an old oak tree and perhaps even an old house on it.

Instantly, we would start thinking about the fun we could have fixing it up. Think of all that open space with peace and quiet. Naturally, there would be a sign saying "For Sale, 25 acres, Reasonably Priced." Buying land is so simple that it's hard to keep from going to the corner real estate office. You don't need to have a lot of money. For a 10 to 20 per cent downpayment you can buy land and go up and sit under that beautiful old oak tree and dream your days away. The temptation is almost overwhelming, but are you sure it is what you want?

There are three basic reasons for buying real estate: to buy a home to live in; as income property; or to buy undeveloped land for its potential to increase in value. (Tax shelters are also involved in buying real estate and will be discussed later in this chapter.)

The criterion for buying a home should not be to make money. It should not be looked at strictly as an investment, although you are looking for quality. It should be looked at as a home you plan to live in, as nicely as possible, for many years. I don't think you should ever look at a house as a temporary home. Many years ago, a young woman told me that she and her husband were buying a certain house until they could afford to buy their dream house. They lived in that house for twenty years! She never really enjoyed living in the house because she always considered it temporary. You should live in your home as though you were planning to live there for the rest of your life.

One of the silliest practices I've ever heard of is to live in a house for ten years and then remodel the kitchen just before you sell it. Why not remodel the kitchen when you first move in and be able to enjoy it! Why wait ten years to do it and then have to leave it! Why put that house in beautiful shape just before you put it on the market! I think you should live in a house as though it were on the market all the time. It's supposed to be your home, enjoy it!

There are other criteria to examine when you think about buying a home. What purpose is the house supposed to fulfill? The house a young family should buy and the retirement home for an older couple are two very different things.

A friend once told me that he was going to buy a retirement home in Monterey, California. He had found the property he wanted and the real estate agent told him that it would increase in value at the rate of about 20 per cent a year. I stopped him, and asked him if he was buying a retirement home or an investment. It's great to have your house increase in value, as long as you realize that it could become too expensive to live in (because of property taxes) and that you might be forced to sell it and move. Profits are nice, but having to move out of your retirement home might not be. When you retire you are living on a fixed income so any investment that could potentially increase your annual costs should be carefully considered. It's important to analyze why you are buying a house and what purpose it is supposed to fulfill.

Tied in with our desire to buy a home, is the idea that we should pay for it as quickly as possible. For some people owning a home that is paid for is the only way to assure peace of mind. This is especially true of many women.

The concept of owning your home, free and clear, has its roots in the word "foreclosure." Prior to the Amortization Act of 1934, you could lose your home if you failed to meet the monthly mortgage payments. Even though you might have been making mortgage payments for ten years you wouldn't get any of your money back. The bank (or whoever held the mortgage) could foreclose—take the house and sell it. They kept all the money from the sale. The Amortization Act of 1934 eliminated this practice. Under the new law, a mortgager can foreclose and sell your house if you miss several monthly payments, but they can only claim the amount of money you still owe on the mortgage. You get the rest. In essence, the government recognizes that you have built up equity in your home. Because of this law, the free-and-clear mentality many of us inherited has become outdated.

Buying a Home

How do you go about buying a home? It's probably the largest single investment you will ever make, so it's important that you go about it in a businesslike manner.

The first thing you have to consider is how much money you can afford to spend, not only in terms of the down-payment, but also in terms of monthly expenses (mortgage payment, property taxes, and maintenance costs). This is a personal decision for every family. It is up to you to determine how you want to spend your money. The classic formula used to be that about 25 per cent of your income should go for shelter, but you may want to allocate more or less than that, depending on your individual desires. In fact, the Consumer Price Index states that the average cost of shelter is now 40 per cent of income. Cam and I wanted our homes to be very nice, so we were willing to cut back in other areas so that we could afford a better home. It cost us a little more than we could easily afford each month, but that money was actually a forced savings that we would get back when we sold or refinanced the house. Remember, however, that the downpayment on the house and monthly mortgage payments are not the only expenses you will incur when owning a home.

There are many other expenses that must be included, such as property taxes, homeowners insurance, maintenance costs, etc. You can spread these costs over the entire year as I mentioned earlier, by setting aside 1/12 of the total amount each month, but they have to be added to your monthly budget.

How can you get the most for your money? This question applies to two areas: the house itself and financial arrangements you are able to obtain. What you desire in a house is, of course, up to your individual tastes and preferences, but one of the most important factors in looking for a house is its location. The neighborhood you select will affect not only the eventual resale value of your home, but also your enjoyment of it. If you look hard enough you may be able to find a modestly priced home in an expensive neighborhood. It takes time and requires investigation, but it's well worth the effort. Finding the right location is very important because you want your home to increase in value, not decrease.

For Cam and me, buying our first home was an exciting venture. We bought a lot at the beach (we lived in Southern California then) and had plans drawn up for a duplex. It was a good design and would have been a good investment for us, but the builder kept increasing his prices, so we got cold feet and sold the lot and the plans. This was a mistake, we later found out, but we were not risk oriented. We thought we couldn't afford to take a chance.

After selling the lot, we decided to look for a house that was already built. There were many new tract homes cropping up in our area and we found two houses that fitted our needs. This was back in the 1940s, so don't be shocked when I mention the prices. One was selling for $12,000 and the other for $16,000. The difference in the monthly payment was only $25, but it was a lot of money in those days and we were afraid we might not be able to afford it. We decided to play it safe and bought the $12,000 house. This was our second mistake. The $16,000 house was a little larger and it was located in a better neighborhood. We wouldn't have outgrown the house as quickly, and we could have made a profit on the house when we sold it. My advice to young couples buying their first homes is to buy the best they can possibly afford. It may be tight for the first few years, but with normal increases in salaries, the payments will get easier every year, and you will have bought value.

You shouldn't look at your home strictly from an investment point of view, but mobility is a fact of life in today's world. When I was a child, no one ever moved, but today families are constantly on the move because of job transfers. You want your home to be a positive investment.

The financial intricacies of buying a home can be confusing so it is in your best interest to learn and understand thoroughly all the details of the transaction. The first step is to find the house and this is often done with the help of a real estate agent. The agent is the liaison between the buyer and seller and is the one who will tell you what the asking price is on the house. This is rarely the final selling price. The potential buyer usually makes what he thinks would be an acceptable counter offer to the owner. This offer may or may not be acceptable to the seller. When a final price is agreed upon, the buyer negotiates with a lending institution to finance the purchase. It is to your advantage to shop around for the best rates available. Perhaps you can afford to make a 10 per cent downpayment, so you must find a lending institution that is willing to loan you the remaining 90 per cent. Shop around for the best interest rates available, because loan conditions and interest rates can vary from one place to another. Mortgage interest rates and "points" (a charge for setting up the loan) are not set figures. Points have nothing to do with the interest rate you are charged on the money you borrow. This charge is usually included in the mortgage loan. Points usually vary between 1 and 3 per cent of the amount borrowed.

Other costs in this financial transaction are the escrow fee and title search fee. When a buyer and seller have agreed upon the selling price and the selling agreement is signed, the buyer is asked to place an amount of money, which is determined by the seller, in escrow. Escrow means a third party holds that money until both buyer and seller have agreed to all of the terms of the sale and the sale is completed. The money held in escrow will be included as part of the downpayment if the sale is completed. If the buyer backs out of the sale the seller may keep the money being held in escrow. A fee is charged for escrow services. A title search must be conducted to verify ownership of the property and to make sure that there aren't any other liens (debts or claims) on the property.

Occasionally, the lending institution will want further verification of the quality of the house you are buying. They may request a termite inspection, or a land survey, and could even go as far as to request an engineering survey of the house's foundations and structural condition. In most states it is the responsibility of the seller to pay for these services and you may find that the cost is part of the buying and selling negotiations. As with any purchase you make, the old adage, "Let the buyer beware," still holds true. It never hurts to be a little suspicious and it is vital that you thoroughly investigate the property you are considering buying.

The real estate agent is, by law, supposed to be impartial, but he is paid by the seller and, naturally, it is to his or her advantage to make as fast a sale as possible. The realtor will assist you throughout the entire transaction and will answer any questions you may have.

Buying a house can get very complicated, so for your own safety I suggest that it might be a good idea to hire a lawyer to examine all the paper work and explain everything to you. The lawyer's fee is small by comparison to the investment you will be making in your home. You don't want any nasty surprises after it's too late to do anything about them, so be cautious.

One thing I would like to warn you about when buying a house (or any property for that matter) is property taxes. When you decide to buy a house, you must ask what the property taxes are. The owner may quote you last year's tax bill, but the problem is that the house may not have been reappraised by the taxing agency in several years. The house you are interested in buying might be selling for a much higher price than the assessment is based on. When someone sells a house, the local assessor's office is aware of it and they immediately update the assessment to the market or selling price, after the sale is made.

How do you determine what the property taxes will be? Call the county or city tax office and ask them what the combined property tax rate is for the area where the house is located. Property taxes are composed of ten or fifteen different tax categories, such as county, city, sewer, hospital, and so forth. The key to buying anything is not to take anything for granted. Always check.

Selling a Home

What about selling your home? Before you sell your old home, you should go out and buy the new home. This sounds scary, but actually it makes a lot of sense. What if I have two monthly payments and two sets of property taxes to pay? Don't worry, you'll manage. If you put your house on the market and it sells, you will only have the usualy thirty days in escrow (finalizing the sale) and then you will have to run out frantically to find a new home. I don't think there should be that much time pressure placed on buying a home.

Cam and I have always bought our new homes first, and then put our old homes on the market and hoped for the best. The first house we had took six months to sell. Yes, we had two payments to make, but we had found a new home that we really wanted. We had plenty of time to do all the remodeling and redecorating we wanted done before we moved in. We took out a short term loan at the bank and were able to get low interest rates because we used our stocks as collateral. When the old house was sold, the money we received from the sale took care of the interim financing (the short term loan). This is what your money can do for you. Don't act too fast when buying a home. Take time to find just what you want.

Many people want to know whether there is any real advantage to going through a real estate firm or whether it wouldn't be just as easy and cheaper to sell their house themselves. In my opinion there are definite advantages to using a real estate firm. Selling property is every bit as complicated as buying and the real estate agent is trained to handle all the negotiations. He insures that all dealings go smoothly and that both buyer and seller are appraised of all the financial details and their individual obligations.

Many people think they can sell their home themselves and save on the agent commission. I don't think this is always wise. The real estate agent earns his/her commission. The agent tries to price your house high enough for a profit, but realistic enough for a sale. He also tries to find the right prospect for your property. He qualifies the prospect. Can this family afford to buy the house? The agent presents you with an offer from the prospective buyer, which you can either accept or refuse. He acts as a negotiator so that you and the prospective buyer can agree on any items, such as furniture and appliances, that are included in the sale of the house. This agreement is in writing so there can be no misunderstanding. The real estate agent is familiar with the lending institutions in the area and will know where and when to open a escrow account and begin the actions necessary to make the sale final. Can an individual do all of this alone? Yes, but it takes time and you have to know what you are doing.

Refinancing

In Chapter 2 I said that borrowing money to buy a home was great, but that refinancing (remortgaging) your home based on its increased value or a large equity build-up was not a good idea except for emergencies. The first statement stands, but the second one is not always true. Refinancing (taking money out of your home) to spend is foolish, but reinvesting that money elsewhere can be a very good idea.

To clarify this, let's look at the true cost of housing. Let's say that your house is worth $85,000 today, and you owe $33,000 on the mortgage. That means you have a $52,000 equity/ownership in your house. You have to consider what that $52,000 could earn if you took the money out and invested it elsewhere. Even if the money was earning a conservative amount of interest, such as 6 per cent, you would have a monthly income of over

$250. If you add this amount to your monthly mortgage payment, property taxes, insurance, and maintenance costs you get a truer picture of what your house is costing you.

We have remortgaged houses three times because we found out that we had a lot of money tied up in those houses that we felt could produce money elsewhere. When you remortgage, your monthly payments go up, but it's actually a blessing in disguise because that money is a forced savings (you are building up the equity in your home). The trick is that you must be able to afford the increase in your monthly payments out of your existing income. You defeat the whole plan if you have to use the money you received from refinancing to cover the increased mortgage payments. Examine this very carefully and you may find, as I did, that all you have to do is cut back a little on other spending in order to be able to manage the increase with no problem.

Refinancing for investment purposes can be an excellent idea, but should be approached cautiously. It is important to research the advantages and disadvantages. For instance, the current interest rate on our mortgage is 7¼ per cent and the house has increased in value since we bought it. Our bank is practically begging us to remortgage the house. We thought about it, but realized that the interest rate would go up to 9¼ per cent if we refinanced. It would be foolish for us to remortgage at that rate, but maybe several years from now the situation will be different and then we'll consider remortgaging.

In order to find out about refinancing your house call the savings and loan associations and banks in your area and find out if they charge to come out and look at your house. Find out what their remortgage rates are. Find out how much the cost (points) of seting up the loan would be. Shop around.

The first time I remortgaged our home, I had a complete proposal worked out on paper that had taken me several months to put together because Cam was working twelve hours a day and didn't have time to see it. The written proposal made it easy for him to see what my idea was. We talked it over and discussed the risks involved. This is the only way to approach an important decision such as remortgaging. You must research it and examine the pros and cons of doing it.

Refinancing just to spend the money is foolish, but sometimes it is necessary, as in the case of my father, Grandpa Schmidt. He had a small house that was paid for, which accounted for a small portion of his assets. His other assets allowed him to be financially solvent and secure for many years. Then, when he was seventy-five he had a stroke and I began dipping into his assets to pay for the services of a housekeeper. I was using his assets to pay for his needs and when they began to run out I remortgaged his house and used the money to continue to provide for the housekeeper. Yes, he was using up all of his assets, but it allowed him to stay in the house he loved, surrounded by friends, until the day he died.

Every circumstance provides a new set of rules in the game of finance. Remortgaging Grandpa Schmidt's house, to spend the money for his benefit, was necessary, and I've always felt it was a wise decision. The accumulation of assets is meant to provide security and sometimes it means having to sell the assets to be able to survive.

Real Estate for Investment

When you talk about real estate as an investment, not a home, you have to consider the quality of the property, the quality of the renter, and how much of your management is necessary, but the major consideration is the fact that real estate is a non-liquid asset. It is not easily converted to cash. It is difficult to sell immediately and you can't sell one room at a time. With a hundred shares of stock you can sell fifty if you need cash quickly, but with a house or building you can't just sell a portion of it.

The other two factors I mentioned, quality of the property and quality of the renter, are also of prime importance. The property should be carefully selected to fit certain requirements. Unless you intend to be a slum landlord it is important that the property you buy be located in an area that has a potential for increased value (an up and coming neighborhood; an old, but stable neighborhood; an established business area; or an area that is attracting business). Your renters should also be carefully selected, because you want someone who will protect, not destroy your investment.

For most of us, the purpose of buying income property is to show an eventual profit. It's important to research thoroughly the property that you are interested in or you could end up losing your shirt—or at least part of it as I did.

I inherited the family home from my father. It was worth about $12,000 at the time and was located in an old and changing neighborhood of Pasadena, California. I had been raised in the house and we had owned it for forty-five years, so for sentimental reasons I couldn't bring myself to sell it. I rented the house to a very responsible-looking woman who was a supervisor for the phone company and who had an adorable little girl. After a couple of years, the rent got slower in coming and I finally realized that I had better get out from under but by that time the house was in a shambles. I ended up selling the house for $9,500, which was more than I expected to get. Who can lose money on real estate in California? Mary Rogers can!

If I had been smart enough, and fortunately we do get smarter as we grow older, I would have looked at the house objectively and asked myself whether I would buy it as an investment. Of course, the answer would have been no. I could have sold it in prime condition for $13,000 or $14,000, but instead I let emotions get in the way and did not ask the question—if I had the money in the bank would I buy this? All of these things must be thought about and analyzed before you take the plunge.

Many people have the mistaken idea that if they buy an apartment building as income property they will get the owner's apartment rent free. Nothing is rent free. If you leased that apartment to another person, you would be able to collect rent from it. If you live in the apartment yourself, you are still paying rent, because you have to take into account the rent money you would receive if the apartment were leased to another person.

Years ago, when I was studying real estate investment, I learned that in order to make a profit from an apartment building you had to have at least four units in the building and live in one of those units yourself. I think this rule still holds true. Having less than four units presents a management problem and decreases the possibility of making a profit. Another thing to remember when buying income property is the age of the building. If the building is going to require constant repairs, it may not be a good investment.

A friend of mine asked me to come with her to see the new apartment building she had just purchased. The building had thirty units and was located at the beach—wow! When we went to see the place I was shocked. It was a slum rental. The previous owner had a manager who had just walked out with some of the rent money, so my friend had to manage this bleak apartment house until she could find a new manager. Good managers are hard to find, especially if you are a small investor. I couldn't imagine that anyone who had anything on the ball would consider living in that hole and managing that apartment house. This is the kind of investment operation that few of us can handle.

I know of only one instance where a friend of mine was able to handle an investment in slum property. He was six feet tall and in excellent physical condition. He was able to collect all the rents when they were due and make all of the necessary repairs on the property. He was also able to handle any fights that might arise and was temperamentally suited to handle his investment. However, I don't think any of us would like to become slum landlords.

When you buy real estate to make a profit you have to realize that it is easy to buy, but not as easy to sell. Just because the property increases in value on paper, it doesn't put money in your pocket. The only time you make a profit is when you sell and receive more cash for your property than the amount you paid. I have known too many people who have become involved in the real estate game to exchange pieces of paper (IOUs) instead of cash. When the property required too much management or whatever, it would go back out on the market for sale. Instead of holding out for cash, these small-time investors would accept a note (second or third trust deed) from the buyer. The note said they had made a profit, but they didn't have any cash in hand. They would finally realize that their actual profit was only a promise of payment on a piece of paper. Too often that piece of paper was worthless. The piece of paper is only as good as the people who sign it. The only time you can say you made a profit is when you have the cash in your hand. Otherwise all you have is an IOU that may or may not be any good.

Real estate is an attractive investment because all you

need is money for the downpayment and then you can usually borrow up to 80 or 90 per cent of the value of the property. All the interest that you pay on that purchase is tax deductible, as are property taxes. There is another tax break on income property (not your home)—depreciation allowance. If you buy property that you rent to others, you are allowed to depreciate the cost of the building over a period of years. This is only permitted on rental property.

The reason for investing in income property, whether rental or undeveloped, is the possibility of potential growth. In an ideal situation you should be able to sell the property for a profit in five to ten years. When you sell the property for a profit it is considered a capital gain and you are required to pay tax on exactly one half of the profit (capital gain). In Chapter 2, I mentioned that you should keep an account of all home improvements you make. The reason for this is that it can help lower the taxes you have to pay on capital gains. When adding the cost of home improvements to the original cost of the house you lower the amount of profit (capital gain) you have made, and there is less money on which you have to pay taxes.

When you own rental property there can be a secondary tax benefit. We've all heard people talking about intentionally taking a loss on an investment to keep their current income taxes down, well, this is how it works. If the rent you are getting for your property doesn't cover the expenses (mortgage, property taxes, maintenance, etc.) and you have to take money out of your own pocket to meet the costs, you are taking a loss on that investment. That loss lowers the taxes you have to pay on your current income. This kind of tax break is only realistic for people with very large incomes.

One reason for buying rental property in the past was that the renter, through his payments, would buy the property for you—mortgage, taxes, maintenance, etc. All you would have to invest would be a small downpayment. It may sound like a good deal, but because of the cost of property today it's not that simple anymore. In most instances the renter is now getting the bargain. The amount you would have to pay in property tax, maintenance, and mortgage for the same living space is probably more than your rent. If you are able to save the difference between the two, you might come out ahead of the family that buys.

Unfortunately, very few people ever do this, but I think it is an idea that many of us should look at more closely.

If you are looking at property as an investment you have to look at the total picture. If you're interested in rental property ask yourself a few questions: Is the property rentable? Will the rent cover all costs? If not, is the loss a benefit to you in lowered taxes? Will the property increase in value? Is there a market for selling? What about unimproved land? When you are buying unimproved property the first question to ask is: How soon will this particular kind of property be in short supply?

Let me tell you about Cam's and my experience with the Kona Coast in Hawaii. A very close friend called me one day and was very excited about a fantastic land development that she knew of. She was anxious to tell Cam and me all about it. She came over with all this audio-visual gear and we sat down to watch slides of this new subdivision in Hawaii, called the Kona Coast. It was only fifteen minutes away from the Rockefeller development. Well, gosh, if it was good enough for the Rockefellers, we were definitely interested. Not only that, but she showed us all these beautiful things that were going to happen to this real estate. We had stars in our eyes and just knew this would be the perfect investment for Cam and Mary Rogers. She showed us the map of the development and two corner lots, which offered the best location because there was going to be a shopping center facing in one direction and a swimming pool facing the other. All it would cost us was a downpayment of $100 apiece on those two lots and $50 a month, but they were going fast so we had to make up our minds immediately. She even had to call her office to make sure they were still available, while we stood by waiting anxiously. We wrote out a check for $200 and went to bed with visions of palm trees, curling surf, and soft trade winds.

In the middle of the night I suddenly came out from under the ether and started wondering about what we had done. I wasn't sure what was wrong, but something was definitely bothering me. As soon as the bank opened in the morning, I put a stop payment on our check and called my friend to tell her we had changed our minds. She thought we were crazy. We weren't. Time has since proved that we made the right decision. Ten years after this incident we saw the Kona Coast and there was nothing there but a lot of lava! There is an unlimited supply of available land on the Kona Coast. If the supply is endless no one is ever going to buy you out for a profit.

A few years after the end of World War II, a number of our friends got involved in an absolutely ridiculous real estate investment. Someone found out that you could become a homesteader in the Mohave Desert and get five acres of free land. Uncle Sam would deed the land to you, free and clear, if you did a certain amount of work on it. Well, you should have seen the fur fly! Everyone made a mad rush to the Mohave Desert, not knowing what they should be looking for, and soon the desert floor was pockmarked with little cement block buildings. There was no running water, no sewer system, no electricity—in short, none of the conveniences people are used to. In no time at all, the thrill of spending the weekend on your *very own* five acres of land went sour.

The important thing to remember is that this land was supposed to be an investment. No one gave any thought to the size of the Mohave Desert. When you have a piece of land as large as the Mohave Desert it is almost impossible to exhaust the supply. Who would buy five acres of land from you when they could get it for free from Uncle Sam? When you buy real estate as an investment you have to ask two questions: Who will I be able to sell this land to and how soon will this land become scarce?

There's another pitfall that I'd like to warn you about and that is buying condominiums, vacation lots, and other property, based on the assumption that something is going to be built on or around it. There are no guarantees that it will happen. A beautiful shopping area, swimming pool, and several other things were promised to us on the Kona Coast deal, but they never came about. Why? Probably because the developer ran out of money. It may be a more expensive way to do it, but I will never buy something that isn't finished. I want to make sure that it is real and not a land developer's fantasy.

Owning property, whether it's your home or income property, can be a marvelous investment, but only if you have researched it very carefully and made sure that it will give you the benefits you think it will. Remember, it is easy to buy property, so be sure you know what you are getting.

Chapter Six Tax Shelters

Americans are obsessed with taxes. We have developed a billion dollar industry of financial geniuses to help us reduce our taxes. There is nothing wrong with trying to keep taxes down, but it shouldn't be your primary concern when selecting investments. An investment should be looked at for quality first and for its tax benefits second. Tax-sheltered investments should only compose a portion of your portfolio of investments.

Why do we have tax shelters? The main reason is to save on taxes, of course, but there are more specific reasons also. You may want to postpone paying taxes due today until retirement when you no longer have a taxable salaried income. Or you may want to reduce the percentage of taxes paid on current income by creating real or artificial (tax deductions) losses. Or you might want to turn some of your current income into a future profit so that you will be taxed at the lower capital gains rate.

Many women who don't understand how some tax shelters work consider them bad investments because the investment may lose money rather than make money. On the face of it this can be true, but the loss is intentional. The function of a tax-sheltered investment is to create losses that lower taxes or to provide a way of postponing taxes until a better time.

There are two inescapable features of tax-sheltered investments. They are often high risk or they lack liquidity (cannot be easily converted to cash). If you try to shelter all of your income you may find yourself locked into a corner with a lot of risky or non-liquid assets. This is a dangerous situation, especially if you are a widow or divorcee. You could find yourself with a great many assets, but no cash to pay off your debts.

Many people who own tax-sheltered investments have no business being involved with them. They think they need tax-sheltered investments because they have an inflated idea of how much tax they are actually paying. There are two basic types of taxes that apply here: income tax, which is based on your annual income and capital gains tax, which requires you to pay taxes on half of the profit you make after selling real estate or certain other investments.

Income taxes are determined on a gradated scale, so the greater your income, the higher the percentage of tax you pay. Most people are unsure about their tax bracket and ask their tax adviser for the information. The adviser might say 32 per cent (or whatever) and you store this information away in your mind. The next time an insurance agent, realtor, or investment adviser asks about your tax bracket you say it's 32 per cent. Without really thinking about it, you accept the fact that you pay 32¢ out of every dollar to Uncle Sam. The advice or suggestions you receive from the insurance agent, investment adviser, and other professionals will be based on that assumption. This percentage is probably much higher than what you are actually paying. Only the very tip of your income is taxed at this high rate; most of your income is taxed at a much lower rate.

This misconception about what you really pay in taxes is exactly why many people who don't need a tax-sheltered investment think they do. Find out what percentage you really pay by dividing the total tax paid by your total income. That percentage is what you really pay in taxes. Unless your income is large enough to warrant tax-sheltered investments, you might be better off paying the regular tax when it is due. Tax-sheltered investments are not a free ride, they all cost something and can be far more expensive than the tax might be on other kinds of investments.

Everyone wants to know how to lower his income tax. How can I have income and not pay income taxes? How can I use my income to make a profit and be taxed with the advantages of a capital gains tax? How can I postpone paying income taxes on money that I am saving for retirement?

There are ways to accomplish all of these objectives. To lower the amount of income taxes you pay on your current income you look for deductions found in investments such as real estate, agricultural investments, and even in such ventures as drilling for oil. These deductions include depreciation allowances on buildings or equipment; interest on loans (mortgages) used to purchase buildings, land, or equipment; property taxes; or maintenance costs on buildings and equipment. These deductions lower your income so there is less money to be taxed. In some instances you don't eliminate the tax, you simply postpone paying it. When you sell the property or building for a profit, you will be taxed with the advantages of a capital gains tax. The catch is that since you have depreciated the building every year, you have lowered the original cost of that building, so when you sell it you will realize a larger profit, which you will have to pay taxes on. When you depreciate property, you are claiming that it is worth less and less every year, but in fact, this may not actually be true. Unless the property is old and run down, you will probably sell it for more than the amount you paid for it. Hence, there is a large gap between what the property is worth on paper and what you sell it for. This is all profit, half of which is subject to capital gains taxes.

These procedures don't actually put money in your pocket. The losses you show are sometimes paper losses and the tax gains are paper gains. All of the investments that allow you these deductions cost money. You can deduct the interest you pay on a mortgage, but you still have to make a downpayment and the deduction doesn't put the money back in your pocket. If you can't afford the investment, the deductions won't be worth much to you.

How can you have income and pay no taxes? By investing in something that allows a depreciation or a depletion allowance or by buying municipal bonds that pay tax free interest. For example, if you invest in an oil well or copper mine, the government recognizes that the oil and copper will eventually run out so it allows you to keep a certain percentage of the income derived from that investment without paying taxes on it.

All of these tax saving maneuvers have merit, but they are designed for the person who is willing to manage her investments carefully and who has solid cash reserves that can support a sagging investment in bad years and still have sufficient income left over to live on. The trouble with some people who get into these tax-sheltered projects is that they usually don't meet these requirements and they don't understand what the project is or the risk involved.

Involvement in some large-scale, tax-sheltered programs, such as oil drilling, real estate developments or cattle feeding, are sold to the investor as a limited partnership. A limited partnership is headed by a general partner, who manages the operation and receives a fee. There can be any number of limited partners, who invest money but have little say in the project's operation. A limited partner can only lose the money he or she has invested in the project and cannot be forced to invest more money and cannot be held liable for any losses or debts that may occur.

One characteristic of limited partnerships is that once you put your money in it may be years before you recover your investment. These investments are not traded on any securities market. If you need to get your money out, *you* have to find a buyer. No broker stands by, ready to handle the transaction. Some of these partnerships do, however, have escape clauses. If illness or death occurs, the general partner may buy your shares at current market value, but there is no guarantee.

A limited partnership allows you to be part of a large scale investment project, but it can be risky and falls into the category that I call "interesting to own." It might be fun to own just ONE of them, but only if you can afford the risks. Limited partnerships are only good investments if the investor is in a high tax bracket.

How can I postpone paying income taxes on money I am saving for retirement? This is a tax-sheltering concept I am in full agreement with for everyone, regardless of their income level. You can postpone income taxes on some of your income by putting it in a company pension plan, Individual Retirement Account (IRA), Keogh Plan or Mini Keogh Plan. These are all tax-sheltered retirement programs and I feel that every person should have a portion of their long-term savings in one of them. If you are participating in a company's pension plan, make sure you understand how it works. You may have a choice regarding the investments that are made.

Company pension plans are great, but what if you are self-employed? In the early sixties, a congressman by the name of Keogh said, if General Motors is able to put money aside for pensions and not pay taxes on that money, why can't a self-employed person (doctor, lawyer, salesman) do the same? (A company plan adds money to your retirement account before any taxes are paid.) Congressman Keogh came up with the Keogh Plan, which allows a self-employed person to invest 15 per cent of his/her *earned* income (not investment income, spousal support, etc.), up to $7,500 per year, in a retirement plan, tax-free. Please note that if a self-employed person does this for himself, the same percentage would have to apply to all of his or her full-time employees. The money earned from this investment will not be taxed as long as it is in the Keogh Plan, but you can't touch it. It is locked up until you are 59½ years old. Then you can take it out of its tax-shelter.

A Keogh Plan can take many forms. It can be made up of stocks, government bonds, mutual funds, or money in a bank account. For example, if you wanted to set up a Keogh Plan funded with stocks, you would go to a brokerage firm and tell them of your intention. Any stocks that you choose to put in the plan would be placed under the custodianship of the Keogh Plan. Any income (dividends, interest) that those stocks produced could not be touched and they would accumulate. Before you set up a Keogh Plan, it is important to know that wherever you plan to invest your money must be approved by the Internal Revenue Service. You can't invest in art, for example.

You have to invest in an institution that has proven itself as secure and reliable. The tax advantages of the Keogh and IRA plans are available through many financial organizations so you have to investigate. How good is the service from a particular financial organization? Have you done business with them before? Is it a national organization that could continue to manage your account if you should move? All these questions should be considered before deciding where you want to establish your retirement plan. You probably have received tons of mail-order literature on all the tax-free plans available, and I would like to caution you about getting involved with them. Investigate all retirement plans thoroughly.

What happens when you decide to take your money out at 60 or later? You haven't eliminated the income taxes on the investment, you have simply postponed paying them. You can either take your assets out at once and pay the taxes, using the advantages of income averaging or you can apportion it out over a period of years. You must, however, take all of your money out of the plan by the time you are 70½ years old. An interesting facet of the Keogh Plan is that if the owner of the plan dies, the beneficiary can chose to accept the assets in the plan as an annuity over a certain number of years. If the beneficiary does this, she or he would not have to pay income taxes on the proceeds from the Keogh plan. If the beneficiary accepts the total assets outright, he or she will have to pay income taxes on them.

I would like to warn you that if you take your money out of a Keogh Plan before age 60, you will have to pay all back taxes, as well as a heavy early withdrawal penalty. You must be cautions when you set this plan up. Just because the plan allows you to contribute 15 percent of your income each year, up to $7,500, doesn't mean you must. There are very few people who can afford to lock up 15 per cent of their income yearly, even if they could save it in the first place. I have seen too many people contribute the full 15 per cent and find themselves borrowing money from the bank, or worse yet, using credit cards excessively because they don't have enough cash to pay for the necessities of life. I think you should try to contribute an amount that you feel comfortable with and can afford to leave locked up. Treat the Keogh Plan with care. Only commit the amount you can afford.

There is also a Mini Keogh retirement plan. This is an attractive plan for the woman who is a part-time worker. For example, if you work for a summer as an independent contractor, and not a salaried worker, you are considered self-employed. There are no income taxes or Social Security taxes withheld from your paycheck. You can put up to $750 a year into a Mini Keogh Plan and not pay income taxes on it. It doesn't make sense to open one of these accounts on a one-shot deal, but if you think that you will probably go back to work for the next ten summers, it could be a good thing to do. There is, however, a ceiling on how high your income can be to be able to participate in the Mini Keogh Plan. Neither of the two Keogh Plans is free. You will be charged custodial fees by the financial organization handling your account, and they can vary, so check it out before you commit yourself. A reasonable custodial fee for a small account ($1,000 to $5,000) might be $7.50 to $10 a year. It's a good idea to find out whether the tax advantage you are getting from a Mini Keogh account is substantial enough to warrant the annual custodial fee.

Another kind of pension plan is the Individual Retirement Account (IRA). The IRA is designed for the person who works for a company that doesn't have a pension program. You can put 15 per cent of your annual income, up to $1,500, tax-free into an IRA account. You can not touch it until you are 59½ years old, and you must take it all out at age 70. Another feature of the IRA is a "rollover" clause. This means that if you receive your pension money when you leave a job, you can put that money into an IRA and it will continue to be tax-free. You have to put the entire amount in, however, and you must do it within sixty days of receiving it.

The IRA was established as a result of strict rules and regulations imposed by the Federal government in 1975 on the management of all company-controlled pension plans. Prior to these government controls there were a growing number of incidences of pension plan mismanagement. We've all heard the horror stories about the man who worked for a company all his life and then when it was time for him to retire found that there was no money in his pension plan. The government is trying to eliminate the possibility of this happening by placing tight restrictions on business, but as a result many companies have decided that it isn't to their advantage to have a pension program. As a result, the need for Individual Retirement Accounts is increasing.

A new feature of the IRA plans is the housewife's retirement plan. This is the first pension program that includes a homemaker in the retirement plan, not just as beneficiary, but in her own name. A man who qualifies for an IRA can increase his total contribution to $1,650 a year by putting $825 in his name and $825 in his wife's name. One thing to keep in mind about the IRA is that the money you put in it must come from "earned" income. It cannot come from interest, dividends, or any other source. It must come from a paycheck.

I want to impress upon you that the Keogh and IRA plans are tax privileges. There is no contract that states you must contribute a certain amount into your program each year. You must be the one to make the commitment to set aside a savings account for the future. Being old in this country has become synonymous with being poor and the government has set up these programs in the hope that the next generation of retired people will actually live what are supposed to be the "golden" years.

Another way of increasing your tax-free retirement benefits is by incorporating. Originally the major reason for incorporating was to lower the income taxes of a professional, such as a doctor, who was earning large amounts of money. At one time there was no ceiling on the percentage of income taxes you could be required to pay, but now, since the 50 per cent tax bracket ceiling on earned income was instituted, the income tax advantage of incorporating is not as important. One of the major reasons for incorporating now is that you are able to greatly increase the amount of money you are allowed to set aside in tax-free retirement plans. For example, the corporate contribution to a retirement fund permitted by the Federal government is 25 per cent of earnings, up to $28,175. This is a huge increase over the allowed individual contribution of 15 per cent up to $7,500. Another advantage to incorporating is that you can charge some life insurance costs and family medical costs against the expenses of the business.

I'd also like to mention one tax saving gimmick that many people get involved in—putting money in their children's names to avoid paying income taxes on any interest that it earns. It works, but do you really want to do it? I can recall long ago I was talking to a dear friend, Mr. Kirchen, and I was telling him that I thought as long as Cam and I were saving for John's education we ought to put the account in John's name to avoid paying taxes. Mr. Kirchen's response was that he was sure John was the finest little boy he had ever seen, but were we sure that down the road we would want all that hard-earned savings to be turned over to John. Legally, the money would be John's to spend in any fashion he wanted. It could be spent sharing an apartment with Susie or buying a pink Porsche. He kindly advised me to keep the money in our family name, paying the small amount of taxes due, because although we would always love John, there could be times when we wouldn't particularly like him. Also, you never know when an extreme emergency will come up and you will need every dime you can lay your fingers on. Save the money, but keep it within your own control. I think it's good advice.

Another type of tax shelter, which I consider a luxury item, is a Clifford Trust. A Clifford Trust is a way to shield high-yield assets from income taxes. You put them in a trust and the income from those assets is given to another person. If you had several children going through college at the same time, you could put a block of high-yield assets, such as corporate bonds, into a Clifford Trust for a minimum of ten years and all the earnings from those assets would go directly to your children. The tax advantage in a Clifford Trust is that the interest would be taxed at your children's tax rate and not yours. This is an advantage in the sense that you would probably be supporting their college education anyway. You could also set up a trust for elderly parents. The Internal Revenue Service has restrictions on how money from a Clifford Trust can be used, so before you consider setting one up, be sure that the purpose for which you want to use it is on the approved list.

A Clifford Trust is a luxury item because there are certain disadvantages that only the very wealthy can afford. A Clifford Trust is irrevocable. Once you set one up you cannot terminate it before the expiration date. You give up ownership of the assets and all their benefits for as long as the trust is in force. You do, however, retain the management of the trust. For example, if the fund is composed of stocks you can sell them, but the money from the sale would go back into the trust. Another factor that you have to consider is that you have no control over what the recipient does with the money. You must be sure that you can afford a Clifford Trust before you set one up.

Tax shelters can be wise investments, but you have to examine the complete picture. You must be sure that you need one and understand exactly how it works. Tax-sheltered investments are complicated and most people have an investment adviser or tax adviser to assist them when setting them up. I advise women whose husbands become involved with tax-sheltered investments to research these investments also and look over the shoulder of their tax adviser to try and find out how the project works. Most husbands do not have the time to follow their investments, a problem with any investment, but with tax-sheltered investments, it can be fatal. Having a tax or investment adviser does not remove all responsibility from you for the management of your hard-earned money. You should be well informed and on top of the situation at all times. It is your money and the only one who will be hurt if it is lost, is you and your family.

Chapter Seven   **Retirement**

Prior to retirement, your life revolves around work and children. These restrictions no longer exist at retirement. What are you going to do with twenty years of retirement life? It's a new phase in your life and it's going to require many adjustments. I think it is just as important to plan what you will do during your retirement years as it is to plan how you are going to finance those years.

Some people think that when they reach retirement age all they will want to do is sit in a rocking chair and watch the world go by. Don't believe it. Very few people have the temperament for a rocking-chair existence. How can you expect to go from an active, stimulating life to a completely sedentary one? It might be a pleasant change for a short time, but I can guarantee that you will get bored with a sedentary life in less than six months. Both you and your husband should develop interests and activities outside of work and children that will help to fill those retirement years pleasantly.

At retirement you are free to do almost anything you want. Your children have left home and you have no job to worry about, so for the first time in your life you can do anything you want and live anywhere you choose. You don't have to accept any limitations. Too many people become rigid in their thinking by the time they reach retirement. They think they have to live within walking distance of their children or near their doctor; or they say they can't afford to make changes. These are all weak excuses. You must revamp your thinking. The only limitations you have are those you place on yourself.

Your needs have changed and the place you lived in during your working and child-rearing years may not fill the needs of a retired couple. You may need a change, but don't rush into it. You have plenty of time. It worries me when a retired couple hurriedly sells their home before really looking around and deciding where they want to go and what they want to do. Explore all the possibilities carefully before you move out of your home. Ask yourself some questions. How deep are my roots here? Do I want to give up what I have and take a chance on something new? Are the activities we enjoy (or new and more exciting activities) available at the new location? If my husband plays golf, is there a golf course near by? Will our children find it easy to come and visit us? Do some serious thinking about your choices. Don't burn your bridges (sell) until you have tried the new idea on for size. You could rent in the new area for a while and rent your own home to defray the expenses. Maybe you should rent in several areas. Take some time to explore. Think of it as an extended vacation. Then go back home and take a good look at what you would be leaving. Get out your pencil and paper and see if the move is financially possible. Your purpose is to find the best spot to live that offers a full and interesting life—not to make money.

It's hard to break the habits of a lifetime and many people have a difficult time keeping the idea of investment out of their decision making. This is particularly true when a retirement home is bought years before retirement. The idea was that if you waited until you retired you wouldn't be able to afford it. This might be true, but the important factor is whether it's what you'll really want when you retire. The mountain cabin is great for vacations when you're 45, but what will it be like when you're 60? Up to the age of 60 we can usually predict what our living patterns may be, but after 60 the road can get a little crooked. Finances change and adjustments are necessary. What looked so rosy a few years before won't look the same when the vacation becomes an everyday thing. The wife particularly should look at this potential retirement situation. Let's face it. She is usually the one who will ultimately have to live in it—alone. Now the questions of where you will live should accommodate the question of whether this choice of retirement home will be acceptable if either the husband of wife should be left alone. Isolation means deterioration and this is the fate of many elderly people.

When Cam and I were exploring a retirement move, it occurred to us that if we were looking for a place that we might want to live in for the rest of our lives, it would be nice to see some action. We found our retirement home on the shores of San Francisco Bay. We can watch a constantly changing panorama from our window. We never get tired of looking out because there is always something going on: boats, planes, fog, people—all kinds of activity. Sitting in a box on a street with no stimulation is slow death for most of us. But then, not everyone's needs are the same. I knew a delightful lady who had been a nurse in a large metropolitan city. She was retired and was visiting friends trying to find a good place to spend her remaining years. We met through a mutual friend who lived in a lovely suburban apartment with green grass, trees, the whole bit. My friend was trying to coax the nurse into sharing the apartment with her. She did, but it only lasted a short time before the nurse packed up and moved out. She moved into a rather seedy downtown hotel and loved it, because that was where the action was. She didn't need the quiet and green grass. She needed busy people and had found where they were and was completely happy.

One thing I'd like to mention is that retirement, like any other stage in life, does not remain the same. You may retire at 60, and find that plans change as you grow older. Sometimes the retirement plans you made at 60 don't fit your needs at 75 and 80. You start to slow down and sometimes need to find a new situation that requires less effort on your part. Take, for instance, the case of Cam's father, Grandpa Rogers. Grandpa Rogers had a big, old house that he owned outright and he and his wife Alyce had lived there all their married lives. They were very happy in the house but times had changed. Grandpa Rogers was now 80 and having to climb up the roof to make repairs didn't make sense. It didn't make Alyce or the neighbors happy either. They were no longer using the entire house and were faced with the necessity of replacing the furnace, which they really couldn't afford to do. The time had come to reevaluate their situation. We talked about it and Grandpa and Alyce admitted that although they loved their home, they wouldn't be that upset to leave it. We started investigating alternatives. There was a new adult community being built fifty miles from their home that offered new apartments that included all maintenance services, etc. There were also a lot of interesting people and activities that would provide needed stimulation for a couple as vital as Grandpa and Alyce. It seemed ideal, but the question was could they afford it? The house was the only asset that Grandpa had, so it was sold and part of the profit was put into a bank account for immediate spending and the balance invested. The return on the investment paid for the total cost of the new apartment and Grandpa still had a small pension to pay for all the little luxuries that make life worth living. It worked out beautifully. They changed their retirement plans to accommodate their new needs.

What would we have done if Grandpa and Alyce had wanted to remain in their home? We would have had to figure out a way for them to be able to afford the maintenance and the cost of having someone keep the place in good repair. Since Grandpa owned the house we could have remortgaged it to come up with the money, but there was also another alternative we could have used. It's called a reverse mortgage and it's a totally new idea, so not all banks and savings and loans will offer it. A reverse mortgage allows the person who has a home that is paid for to borrow money, usually a monthly amount, against the equity in his or her home. The bank or savings and loan that sets up the reverse mortgage charges interest on the money you borrow, but it is less than you would pay if you remortgaged your home and it does not have to be paid until the house is sold or transferred into an estate. I think this is an excellent program and I hope it will become more widely used because it is not unusual that at some point an older couple will have to start using their principal to be able to live decently. A reverse mortgage is one way to do this, but very slowly.

What I've tried to show is that there are almost always alternative (and sometimes better) ways to arrange your finances to fulfill a need. Don't ever lock yourself into a situation you can't get out of. Try to keep your finances as flexible as possible. If your needs change, your finances need to change to fit those needs. This brings up something that I'd like to caution you about and this is lifetime care. By lifetime care I mean buying into an institution that will provide you with a total living situation, including medical care, for as long as you live. Many religious organizations have set up these facilities and you pay a flat fee to join. There are also many private concerns (not affiliated with any religion) that have been established in recent years that provide lifetime care. I approve of paying for lifetime care, *if* you understand that the greater portion of your total money shouldn't be turned over to an institution. If the cost of buying in will not consume more than 50 per cent of your total assets, then I feel you could take the risk. Risk, what risk? There's always a risk. If inflation increases, the cost of everything you might want to do, outside of the room, board, and medical care you are buying, may become more expensive than you can afford. You could become limited in your activities and life wouldn't be much fun. Far too often people scrape the bottom of the barrel to get the funds together to buy lifetime care because of the fear that they'll run out of money before they die. They become locked into a very limiting situation. They have no funds to spend on anything that would break the monotony. Lifetime care is a luxury for those who can afford both the cost of buying in and still have enough to spend on the luxuries of life.

Another living arrangement that I'd like to discourage is the practice of retiring in a foreign country to lower your cost of living. Most of the countries that offer a lower cost of living are politically volatile. We've all read stories about Americans living abroad and losing property that they thought they owned. It can be a very chancy situation. I will admit, however, that sometimes it can work. A friend of mine who was caring for an invalid husband decided that she ought to move to Mexico where she could afford to hire adequate help to care for her husband. The move was successful because she planned it carefully. She investigated the project thoroughly before doing anything and she even learned to speak Spanish. But, I think my friend was lucky. Make sure you have examined the risks before you make a move.

If you are considering living abroad, a beginning checklist might include checking to see if you can still receive your retirement benefits while living in another country; you can receive Social Security benefits, but not Medicare or Medicaid. What are the medical facilities like in this other country? How does the cost of living compare with that in the U.S.? Housing may be cheaper, but what about the cost of food, gas and electricity? Do you understand the culture of the country and would you feel comfortable living in it? Do you speak the language or could you learn it easily? Is the country politically stable? If a new government comes into power, would foreigners be forced to leave or lose their possessions? You should consider all of these things before you commit yourself. It would be a good idea to visit the country and maybe rent for a while to see if it is really what you want.

I like the idea of living abroad if the purpose of the move is seeking an exciting adventure, but I get very concerned when the motivation for moving to a foreign country is the supposed advantage of a lower cost of living. I fear that there is an added cost that can't be measured in dollars. It is still a foreign country and it may never feel like home.

Finding the right place to live is only half the battle in retirement. It's a new phase of your life and it may require many adjustments. When Cam and I pulled up stakes and moved 400 miles away from our old home I had a terrible time adjusting. Cam weathered the move much better than I did and I finally figured out why. A woman *lives* in the old neighborhood. The man comes home to sleep during the week and enjoys two days a week during the weekends. He really only visits the neighborhood, whereas his wife lives there. There was another adjustment that I had to make when we retired and this one was quite a shock. When we moved into our retirement home Cam mentioned that he thought one of my plants should be moved to another wall! How could he? What right did he have to change anything? Well, he had all the right in the world—it was his home too. The first thing I had to do was give Cam his house. It was not easy and even years later I still find myself occasionally gritting my teeth.

For many of you, retirement will be the first time since before the kids were born that you've had to really live together—just the two of you—and let me tell you sometimes it may not be easy! Take for example, the experience of some good friends of mine, Mary and Jack. Mary called me in an absolute fit one day to tell me that Jack was being totally unreasonable by refusing to let her continue the painting lessons that she enjoyed. Goodness, I thought, what's going on? For thirty years Jack had brought home his paycheck and given it to Mary who did a remarkable job of money management. All of a sudden, the first month after he retired, Jack was sitting by the window waiting for the Social Security check, the pension check, and all their interest and dividend checks to come in the mail. He had decided to become the money manager. What a shock! During the thirty years of their marriage he had paid little attention to the family money and now, out of the blue, with no experience, he was going to handle it all. Well, this could be just fine, but he'd decided that they should live far differently than in the past and that certain things would have to be cut out of the budget. Of course, the first thing to go was Mary's painting class. How did Mary and I solve this problem? We had to put together a budget to prove to Jack that certain expenses could be covered by their income. We listed in great detail every item of monthly expense, including the dinners out, club dues, painting lessons, and so forth and then we added it all up to see how close we were to their retirement income. The budget worked and Jack was able to see that they could easily afford the little extras, such as painting lessons. You may have to do this too, because men will often find it difficult to look at their new financial status realistically. To them, living on a fixed income means that they are now poor, which is not necessarily true. The moment that incomes become fixed, a detailed budget must come into being, so that you can really look at your expected costs and determine together what values you place on your spending. The old saying "Retirement offers twice as much time to spend and only half as much money" is often true.

It is up to you to get the most out of your money, but don't needlessly deprive yourselves.

Men often go through what I call "retirement shock." Their identities are often closely tied to their jobs and when that identity is taken away, they have a hard time adjusting. That loss of identity should be replaced with something else. A smart couple realizes this and begins to replace that identity before retirement occurs. In retirement, the golf club dues, the yacht club, the bowling league, etc., can not be looked at as the luxuries they were during the working years. They could be a necessity and a smart wife should realize that they might actually take the place of doctors' bills. Perhaps there is something that you or your husband or both of you might enjoy doing together. This is great, but don't take the pleasure out of it by making your hobby a full-time job.

I knew a retired couple who were rock collectors. They enjoyed spending their days in the country looking for unusual (and sometimes valuable) rocks. One day when they were in a rock shop, the owner approached them about possibly buying him out. The prospect excited them, so they decided to buy the shop. This was going to be such fun, but something happened. Neither one of them knew anything about running a business. They were working harder than they ever had before. The business was booming, but once the stock was sold what did they do? Merchandising is buying and selling the right product for a price that makes a profit. Sounds simple, doesn't it? It is an art and it takes a lot of work. My friends had no idea of what they were getting into. Rock collecting was no longer an enjoyable hobby, it was a demanding *job*. I think this is crazy! Don't retire to a killing occupation. Wouldn't it have been more fun for my friends to become investors in the shop rather than owners? Then they could have participated in the business, but only as much as they wanted.

Retirement offers many choices. You can do anything you want. I think a good definition of retirement is, "the time to do all the marvelous things you never had time for before." It should be a time for exploration and new adventures in living. Anything is possible, if you have planned for your retirement. Then your retirement years *will* indeed be "golden."

Chapter Eight   **Divorce**

Usually when a woman tells me that she and her husband
are getting a divorce she is in one of three frames of
mind. She either wants to take him to the cleaners for
every penny she can get; or she doesn't want anything,
except out of the marriage; or she wants a divorce but
feels guilty about asking for any of "his" money. All of
these attitudes are unrealistic. It's almost impossible to
clean a man out in divorce anymore and to ask for nothing
or next to nothing after years of marriage is stupid and
demeans the efforts you have expended in that marriage.
Whether or not you earned a paycheck during your married life, you have worked and have certainly earned whatever you receive as a settlement.

Divorce is a legal process to discontinue a marriage and
regardless of how emotion-charged it can be, you must

treat it as the business transaction it really is. As I've said before, emotions and financial decision-making do not mix and this is never more true than during a divorce. Do your crying at home and the rest of the time try to be as businesslike as you can.

I have counseled many women who were contemplating divorce, in the midst of divorce, or just emerging from divorce and almost 100 per cent of the time the first thing I find I have to do is rebuild her feeling of self-worth. I am aghast at the low value that women place on their efforts in a marriage, but I guess I shouldn't be. After all, it has been drummed into our heads for as long as we can remember that a woman's contribution to a marriage is not worth much since she doesn't bring in a paycheck, or if she does, it's so small that it doesn't count. THIS IS NOT TRUE! If a woman gets nothing else from this book, I want her to finish it knowing that her contributions and her worth are so vast that they can't even be calculated.

Through your labors, energy, and concern for your husband and children you have been an *equal* partner in your marriage. It has been the combined efforts of both husband and wife that have raised a family, supported the husband in his career, and enabled him to further his ability to increase his earning power and potential. A wife must acknowledge her efforts and accept that part of the marriage that has been her achievement, even though she may never have earned a dollar.

There is no time in a woman's life when it is more important for her to stand up seven feet tall and say, "I have been an equal partner in this marriage," than during a divorce. Why is it so terribly important then? Because during the course of a divorce she will be constantly reminded that her husband is the source of all money. She must be made aware of her own contribution. It is "our" money not his. Otherwise what happens is that she becomes the victim of an insidious campaign to force her to accept an inadequate settlement. She is not treated as though she is an equal partner in the marriage, but more as a parasite in that marriage. Often, her contributions are so belittled that she becomes completely demoralized and will sign anything just to get the divorce over. This is tragic. Don't let it happen to you. You know that without you, your husband wouldn't be where he is, so stand up seven feet tall and let him and everyone else know it too!

The second thing I have to do when a woman comes to see me, is convince her that although a divorce may start out as a friendly, mutual separation, it almost never stays that way. I can almost guarantee that as soon as you start negotiating the division of the assets that you have acquired during your marriage, what started out as a friendly little divorce will quickly turn into a snarling confrontation. I am not exaggerating. It may be hard for a husband to write a check for alimony and child support, but nothing will hurt as much as dividing the assets. All of a sudden, he will start reminding you that he earned all the money, and that he doesn't have to share any of it with you. He's wrong, of course, because in most states he does have to share the assets, but don't expect him to like it. This is the time to keep patting yourself on the back, saying "Yes, I did earn half of this money!"

The first thing to consider when thinking about a divorce is where you live. Divorce laws are governed by the state and they can vary considerably. You must find out what your state's divorce laws are and what your rights are under those laws. Some of the places where you can go to get this information are: the State's Commission on the Status of Women; the National Organization of Women (NOW); The League of Women Voters; and the American Association of University Women. I also strong suggest that any woman going through a divorce go down to the courthouse and attend several court sessions on divorce cases. You will find out not only how the divorce process works, but also how the judges arrive at their decisions. It's a good idea to take a friend along for these sessions because when you are going through an emotional experience such as divorce it is sometimes difficult to concentrate on what is going on around you. You need a second set of ears to make sure you don't miss anything. If you prepare yourself for the court session in advance, it won't be such a shock when you find yourself before the judge.

Aside from these two things, finding out about the divorce laws in your state and attending court sessions, you should hire a lawyer. There is no acceptable reason for not having your own lawyer. No matter how amiable the divorce is, emotions will become involved. You need your own advocate. One lawyer cannot function as the attorney for both husband and wife. The divorce process is a process of negotiation and each partner needs a spokesman who will have their best interests in mind.

Your selection of a lawyer is vitally important. Most areas have a local office of the Bar Association that can direct you to several lawyers who specialize in divorce. Make an appointment to meet with one of them; this doesn't mean you have to hire that person. During the time of negotiation you will need someone who gives you confidence and with whom you can communicate easily. If a lawyer doesn't fulfill these two qualifications, you don't want him/her. The attorney's first role is to explain the local divorce laws to you and how the process works. Then he/she should try to find out as much about the financial aspects of your marriage as possible. This will give your lawyer clues as to how to proceed. Your lawyer may be the most important person in your life when you are going through divorce proceedings, so make your selection carefully.

If you are the party instigating the divorce, your lawyer will give you certain papers to fill out to inform your husband that you are filing for a divorce or legal separation. Then the court will be informed that you are starting divorce proceedings and you will have to pay certain fees for the service of the court.

Your attorney will need to obtain a monthly budget from you, based on your husband's income. He will also need to know what all the family assets are. Both of these financial statements must be as accurate as possible. Your attorney knows nothing about you. You are his source of information. Hence, he can only be as good as you are. You must do all the homework, because everything your lawyer does will be based on the information you provide for him.

When you put together your monthly budget it should include all your expenses. If you have children, you must consider their specific needs, particularly if they have any special ones, such as weekly allergy shots or a problem that requires special education. The budget should also include all annual expenses such as school tuitions, school clothing, car insurance, home insurance, medical insurance, transportation expenses, home maintenance expenses and income taxes on spousal support (your ex-husband will not be taxed on the money he gives you in spousal support, but you will be, so put it in your budget). These annual expenses should be divided by twelve and then added to your monthly budget.

Another expense that I think is important—one that most attorneys don't consider—is a life insurance policy on your ex-husband. If you are still dependent on another person's income (your ex-husband's) then you should insure that income. If your ex-husband should die, who is going to pay your alimony and child support? There should be enough money in your budget to be able to purchase a term policy on your ex-husband's life. This will insure the money that you should receive during the time your ex-husband will be supporting you and your children. This budget is very important and should be worked out very carefully. The next step is to put together a list of all your family's assets. Sit down and try to think of all the things that your family owns. For example, what is the market value of your house? What do you think your furniture and possessions are worth? Is there cash value in your husband's life insurance policy? Do you own any investments? If you have not been paying attention to these financial details, you may be in trouble. Try to gather as much information as you can so your attorney can do his job well. If your husband is a frugal man, he may have investments or a savings account that you are not aware of.

The primary source for much of the information you need is your income tax statements. They should detail the source of your family's income. Don't hesitate to go to your husband's accountant and ask for copies of the tax returns for the last five years. This is not being underhanded or sneaky. If you signed those income tax statements, they are as much yours as your husband's. The forms should give you a fairly accurate picture of what your family's finances are. But what happens if you have been filing separate tax returns? Can you still get copies of your husband's returns? No, but the idea of getting copies of his returns is probably only necessary for the woman who files a joint return with her husband and hasn't been paying attention to the family's finances. If she files her own return, she is more likely to be aware of family finances in general. Once you determine what it costs you to live (from your budget), the sources of your family's income, and the assets you own, you can create a complete picture for your attorney that he can use to successfully negotiate a fair divorce settlement for you.

What if when you start gathering this material you find that there's a large sum of income that you can't account for. Let's say that you have found that the family's annual income is $50,000 (including paychecks and income from other assets) and that your taxes run about $10,000 annually and that you spend about $2,000 a month for living expenses. That leaves about $16,000 you can't account for. Start looking for the $16,000. The most logical possibilities are any investments your husband might have (savings accounts, stocks, bonds, real estate, etc.). This is the work that you do to make your attorney effective. He must be able to deal from a position of strength and knowledge. He also has the power to subpoena, and if you have an idea where that $16,000 might be but you are not sure, he can subpoena records to investigate your suspicions.

One asset that is not usually considered in divorce proceedings is your husband's Social Security benefits. Rarely does anyone consider the fact that during all your married life, your family's income has been subject to Social Security taxes. Unless you have been married for ten years, you have no claim to any Social Security benefits. If you get a divorce after nine years you are not entitled to any Social Security benefits. I think this fact should be brought up during divorce negotiations, but it rarely is.

Your husband may also have a pension or profitsharing plan with his company. This is usually locked up until termination of employment or retirement. This money should also be included in your list of assets.

Your attorney will use all the information you have gathered to negotiate for two things: spousal suport (commonly referred to as alimony) and child support. These are two separate obligations and should never be discussed in the same breath. Your husband has a financial responsibility to you and an entirely different financial responsibility to his children. A third area of negotiation is the division of all assets the two of you have acquired during your marriage.

Even if you live in a community property state, the divorce settlement will probably include some division of assets (either the assets themselves or cash from the sale of those assets) and spousal support for a fixed number of years. Spousal support is rather straightforward and is based on your husband's income and the monthly budget you present. The division of assets is more involved. I feel that a woman should try to receive a cash settlement, if at all possible. The reason for this is that many assets can become a liability to the divorced woman because of her reduced financial status. You have to examine each asset separately and determine whether it is appropriate to your needs. For instance, you would not want a tax-sheltered investment, such as a piece of undeveloped land, because you probably won't have a large enough income to shelter and you would have to continue to pay property taxes on the land. You have to understand the consequences of accepting certain assets as a settlement. Do the assets produce income? You can't afford to have assets that don't. If you sell the assets after the settlement, will they bring the price stated in the settlement agreement? These are all things to consider before accepting any asset as part of a settlement. A block of high-yielding corporate bonds might be an asset you would want. Check everything out carefully.

The biggest trap many women fall into is accepting the family house as their settlement. The reason I say it's a trap is because you have to face the fact that the same income that supported one household will now have to support two. Your standard of living will have to change. You may not want to give up your house because it's your home, and you love it. Also, some women feel it may not be good for the children to lose their father and their familiar neighborhood at the same time. But, can you afford to live in the house on the amount of money you are going to receive from your ex-husband or from any job you might have? You have to remember that the monthly house payment, insurance, maintenance costs, and property taxes are all part of owning a house. These expenses will remain the same, but your income will be greatly reduced. Remember also that the true cost of that house includes the amount of lost income locked up in the equity (ownership) of that house.

You have to examine the consequences of accepting the family home as part (or all) of your settlement. The amount of money you are asked to accept as part (or all) of your settlement is the market value of your home, minus the unpaid balance on the mortgage. Is that what you will really get? What often happens is that within a short period of time, the divorced woman, who is rarely able to earn a substantial income of her own, realizes that spousal support and child support will not support the cost of living in the family home so she must sell it. Now right off the top of what she gets for the house she must deduct the costs incurred in selling it—usually around 10 per cent of the selling price—and then she has to pay a capital gains tax on half of the profit she makes.

When these two expenses are deducted from the selling price of the house she discovers that what she receives is a lot less money than she was supposed to get from the divorce settlement. You have to look at the cost of selling a house before you are sure that you are receiving half of the family's assets. Perhaps instead of accepting the house as your half of the settlement, the house should be held in "tenants-in-common" with your ex-husband. This way, both of you would own half of the house and then when it is sold—maybe several years later—a final settlement would be made, with both parties sharing the cost of selling and the capital gains taxes, and then dividing the remaining profit. If you decide to do this, I think it is a good idea to set a time limit for selling the house when the tenants-in-common agreement is signed. It should be in the agreement that the house will be sold in two or five years or perhaps when the youngest child goes away to college. This way, both parties are in agreement, and neither of them can refuse to sell the house when the time limit expires. Summing up, I don't think a woman should accept the family house as her settlement unless she is aware of the costs she will have when she sells it. Make sure you know what you are getting.

You may encounter a problem when getting a divorce settlement if all the family's assets are tied up in your husband's business. He has control of the family assets and therefore control of your income. Is there a way to get out of this situation? I know of one woman whose husband was a partner in a legal firm and he told her that there was no way he could put a dollar-value on the partnership. This isn't true. At the time of death there is always a way to place a value on assets, so she forced her husband and his partner to put a dollar-value on the partnership. As a result, they had to borrow money to pay her divorce settlement. If you have been married for many years and your family's assets are locked up in your husband's partnership, you are entitled to your fair share. Sometimes you have to stand up seven feet tall and make your demands known. There has to be a way to place a value on anything.

I think a divorced woman should try to start her new life with as clean a slate as she can. One of the smartest women that I know was getting a divorce and decided not to keep the family house. She had grown up in a small town and decided that she would like to live in one again, so she selected a small town that had good schools, opportunities for employment, and a nice warm atmosphere. It was also a town where she could buy a nice home for a modest sum that she could afford. When you get a divorce your lifestyle changes. Make it a change for the better.

Child support is the other key element in the process of negotiating a divorce. Generally, this is not an area that is strongly contested by the man. The only point that gets touchy is how much money a husband should pay in child support. In most instances, a man recognizes his responsibility towards his children and is willing to pay for their support. The reason the amount of child support becomes a problem is that he wants the money to go strictly to the support of his children and doesn't want his wife to benefit from it. If it's a large amount, the husband might feel that his wife is the one who is really getting the money. This hangup is especially prevalent in an unpleasant divorce. It's difficult to combat this attitude, but you have to stick to your guns, because child support payments are rarely sufficient to really support a child.

Most child support is awarded in the form of a fixed monthly amount, but I feel very strongly that a child should benefit from his natural father's financial success. A divorce does not mean that the kids are no longer his problem. He is getting a divorce from you, not his children. Rather than a fixed monthly sum, I think child support should be a percentage of the father's income, for two reasons: as I said, children should benefit from their father's success and a fixed amount does not take into account inflation or the increased financial needs of the child as he/she grows older.

In most states the obligation of child support stops at age 18. Now, most mothers know that few children are able to be on their own at that age. Even when they are away at school there are times when they need a *home.* If child support stops at 18, what then? This is the big question that worries many women who have been smart enough to look ahead. Naturally, if there's no alternative, you struggle along doing the best you can, but if provisions have been made for your ex-husband to provide additional support for the education of his children, some of that money should be used to help maintain the home that those children still need even though they are away at school. Often, at the time of divorce, trusts are established to provide educational funds for the children. It is at that time that you should ask that a certain amount of that money be marked for assistance in maintaining the home. This is a unique idea and one that may cause high blood pressure for your ex-husband. There's no guarantee that you can get this additional support, but for the child's sake I think it's worth a try.

Since we're on the subject of children let's discuss some of the problems that can occur with children when a divorce takes place. I won't attempt to go into the emotional stresses placed on them because that depends upon individual family circumstances. The problem with children is that whenever there is a divorce or death, they often suspect that Mom now has "money." The only realistic response to this situation is to develop "child deafness." I'll explain this in a moment. There is no way that your children can understand what it means to live on a fixed income. A new widow or divorcee has to assume total responsibility for her financial future and I don't approve of the idea of discussing finances with children. They cannot truly understand your new financial status, so it is wrong to consult them.

One of the hardest adjustments you'll have to make after a divorce is assuming the role of the strong parent. You will have to make some serious financial decisions, and most likely, your children are going to have to adapt to a new and different standard of living. They will not be happy about this and might even try to blame you for the divorce. They may make some unkind statements, such as "Dad never would have left if you had been a better wife." You have to ignore these remarks by developing "child deafness." This is the reverse of "parent deafness," which children sometimes use when they don't want to listen to their parents. Let them say anything they want, but pretend you don't hear them. Don't explain anything until you get over the hump. Eventually, they will recognize your strength, and realize that they are wasting their time. Don't argue with them, just smile. You don't have to discuss your finances with your children.

Going through a divorce is a difficult ordeal for the entire family and children aren't always equipped to deal with the changes a divorce can cause in their own little worlds. If you recognize this, you can prevent a lot of unnecessary arguments, especially about money. Putting your children on their own budgets will help them adjust to their "new" life much faster than screaming about money all the time. You will also teach them the fundamentals of financial responsibility in the process.

I knew of one young divorcee who was scared silly by her new financial situation. As soon as her children came home from school, she would start screaming at them about using the phone and consuming all the Cokes and cookies. I noticed this when I was visiting her one afternoon and realized she had to do something about this situation or her children would soon start to hate her and she would end up a nervous wreck. I helped her put together a detailed budget and showed her that she could afford to set aside $40 a month for little extras for the kids, including the phone and Cokes and cookies. She told the kids that they had to learn to budget the $40 so that it would last an entire month. This was an important step for this woman because, although her children realized that money was tight, they didn't understand how it affected them.

One of the most foolish things that a divorcee can do is to build up a false sense of security for her children. She may not want her children to be frightened by the new financial situation so she tries to pretend that nothing has changed and that there is enough money to do all the things they did before the divorce. She ends up spending all her cash settlement in no time and the end result is that the kids really have something to worry about now—the support of a destitute mother. Children are usually marvelously adaptable creatures and they can adjust easily to a new situation if they know what their limitations are. Remember, security does not have to be a big house and a lot of luxuries. Security should be a loving parent and the feeling of home, even if it means sleeping bags on the floor of an apartment.

I can not stress enough to the divorcee that her standard of living will have to change. Even if she is lucky and receives generous alimony and a large settlement, that money will not last forever. A $50,000 settlement may seem like an enormous amount of money to you, but if you spend it indiscriminately, it will be gone before you know it. Alimony and child support are both temporary. I think it is far wiser to re-evaluate your lifestyle and make some changes. Try to adjust your budget so you can live on the alimony and child support for as long as they last. Put your "lump sum" settlement in a safe investment where it will grow. You will probably never have that much money in your hands again. Think of it as your future and don't piddle it away. Use the time while you are still being supported by your ex-husband to develop the skills you need to be able to support yourself.

Learning to support yourself is the most important change you will have to make. You are now alone. Your whole life has changed and you're going to have to learn to fend for yourself. What do you want to do? Sit down and take a good, hard look at the skills or talents you possess and think about how they could be applied to specific jobs. You may find you need to invest some time and money in acquiring certain job skills. If you feel you need to go back to school, do it. You may have several years when you will still be supported by your ex-husband, so put your time to good use.

If you don't learn to support yourself, the results can be disastrous. Let me give you an example of what happened to my friend Jane. Her divorce settlement included $800 a month in spousal support for four years and $150 a month in child support for each of her three children until they reached eighteen. The first year after her divorce she received $1,250 a month in support from her ex-husband and managed to get along quite well. The second year one of her children turned 18, so she lost $150 a month in income. The third year her second child turned 18 and she lost another $150 a month. The fourth year was the last year she would receive $800 a month in alimony and the following year her youngest child turned 18. After five years she had no income. Jane should have taken a close look at her financial situation right after the divorce.

Another friend of mine, Sharon, decided to go back to school to become a nurse after her divorce. I encouraged her to spend four years studying full-time, rather than working part-time and taking longer to finish her schooling. It wasn't easy for her to do this. She and her children really had to watch their pennies during those four years, but when she graduated from nursing school she was totally self-sufficient. She planned ahead for her future and was financially secure by the time her ex-husband's support ended.

Many women lack self-confidence when they are faced with the prospect of finding a job. They believe they have no talents and even fewer skills. This pessimistic attitude is guaranteed to get you nowhere. Maybe the problem is that you have never thought of yourself as a "working woman" and you haven't the slightest idea of what you might be able to do. One way to find out is to job-hop. Allocate a certain time period, say one year, to finding out what types of jobs are available and might interest you. Naturally, you won't be able to get a high-level job at first, but you'll be able to gain some valuable experience. Perhaps you've thought that you might enjoy a fashion-oriented job. You probably couldn't get a job as a buyer in one of the department stores, but you could get a job as a sales clerk. Once you're on the inside, you can find out what a buyer really does and what you have to do to become one. If you discover that it is not what you'd like to do, move on to something else.

The trick is getting inside a business to find out what jobs are available and what skills are required to get the "good" jobs. There are many "entry-level" jobs that require little or no experience. Don't limit yourself. You have several years to become self-supporting, but don't waste them. If you don't take advantage of this opportunity you could find yourself on welfare or marrying any man who comes along simply because he can pay your rent.

One other thing that I would like to mention about this re-educational period is to avoid letting yourself get defeated by insignificant problems. If you go back to school and find you are having trouble with a particular subject, don't waste your time struggling with it, go out and hire a tutor to help you. If you allow yourself to get discouraged at the beginning, you'll never accomplish your objectives. It is natural that you may have a few problems at first. Don't expect miracles to happen, just go slow and easy and the little frustrations of your new role will work themselves out.

No one gets married with the idea that they will get a divorce, but it seems to be becoming an increasingly prevalent occurrence. I found out recently that the county I live in has one of the highest divorce rates in the country and I began to wonder why. I realized that relationships between men and women haven't really changed much since I was a young girl, but women's reactions to those relationships have changed. Divorce was almost unheard of thirty years ago—it wasn't socially acceptable. A woman didn't seek a divorce from an alcoholic, a woman-chaser or a wife-beater; she coped. Today's woman refuses to cope with a bad marriage. She has begun to realize that she has other options and that she doesn't "have" to put up with a situation that is making her miserable. In some instances, however, women fail to see and plan for the reality of having to support themselves.

The truth of the matter is that some women cannot afford to get a divorce. There is not enough money to finance a divorce. A young woman came to see me and the first thing she said was that she wanted a divorce from her husband. After looking over the family's financial situation, I told her she couldn't afford a divorce. She had three young children and hadn't held an outside job in ten years. Her husband earned an average wage, but they were up to their ears in debt. If she got a divorce, her husband would only have enough income left after paying all the bills to pay her a pittance each month and child support would be non-existent. She would have no money to live on and any immediate job she could get would not bring in enough income to support herself and her three children. If she divorced her husband, she would have to go on welfare. There just wasn't enough money to go around.

What do you do in a situation like this? Obviously, you can't get a divorce immediately, but if you really want one you have to resolve the financial situation first. You cope with the circumstances until you can "afford" a divorce. As strange as it may seem, many "dead" marriages have been revived at this point. Money, or the lack of it, is a major cause of marital problems, but sometimes when a wife jumps in to help resolve those financial problems, the marriage begins to blossom again. It's definitely worth a try. You must have loved your husband when you married him, and perhaps you still do. Your marriage could be suffering because of the morass of financial worries that have you at each other's throat.

Getting a divorce is not as simple as it sounds and unfortunately, a wife is usually hurt the most. She is the one whose life is turned upside down. She is at a disadvantage in the job market and usually has to adjust to a lower standard of living. Sure, a husband doesn't get off scot free (if he is the responsible type and pays what he is supposed to) but he retains the ability to make money. A divorce doesn't affect his earning power and chances are he will continue to make more and more money, whereas his wife cannot really hope to achieve the success that he can (especially if the divorce takes place in middle age or later). There are exceptions to the rule but they are few and far between. Also, even though the court may say that your ex-husband has to pay you spousal support and child support, that doesn't mean that he will. The fact is that 40 per cent of all child support payments are in arrears and alimony is in about the same state and there is not much you can do about it. Well, you say, I can sue! But can you? Lawyers often demand payment in advance for their services and unless you have money how are you going to sue? This is why you have to know what you are doing when you go to a lawyer and start talking divorce.

If you start divorce proceedings you have to maintain a close relationship with your lawyer. If you feel that things are not going the way they should or that your lawyer is not really working for you, put a halt to the whole proceeding. You have that right, but most women don't realize it. If the divorce negotiations cannot be resolved among you, your husband, and the two lawyers, you have the option of throwing yourself on the mercy of the court. You leave the decision making to an objective third party, a judge, with the hope that he will arrive at a fair settlement for both of you. Then when the divorce is over, lift up your head and go out and see what the world has to offer you and, even more important, what you have to offer the world. You are unique and no one in the world can do things in exactly the same way you can. You are going to live to be 80, so don't waste a minute of your time.

I'LL LET YOU SEE MY
WILL, IF I CAN SEE YOURS...

Chapter Nine **Death**

I would venture to say that the vast majority of people in this country, both men and women, don't have the slightest idea of what happens when a person dies. Many of us are familiar with the terminology associated with death, such as wills, codicils, probate, trusts, and executors, but how many people really know what these terms mean? We all die eventually, so why do we persist in ignoring the legal ramifications of death?

Most men die before their wives, yet many women fail to accept this fact until death occurs. It doesn't make sense to dwell on death, but a woman must prepare herself for the strong possibility that she will outlive her husband. There are two aspects of death that will be covered in this chapter: planning for it and what you have to do when it happens.

Planning for death simply means legally arranging for the distribution of assets before death occurs. Obviously, this can involve many different beneficiaries, but we will narrow it down to what can take place between husband and wife. The first step in planning for death is to write a will. Both husbands and wives should have their own wills. Regardless of any other legal arrangements you make for the division of your estate (trusts, etc.), you should also have a will. Anything you can do to eliminate any confusion or trouble at your death is important. Even if this means writing a letter explaining your wishes on various items of furniture or jewelry—things that might not go into a will, but that should be given to those most likely to enjoy their use. Better yet, I think it is a sensible idea to give these things to loved ones as you get older, rather than hold on to possessions you no longer need or enjoy.

Many husbands and wives have arranged their affairs to insure that if one of them dies the surviving partner receives everything. This is fine, but what if you both die at the same time? You must have a will that names an heir in the event that both of you die at the same time. If you don't do this the state in which you live has a formula that is used to determine how your estate will be divided. They have no way of knowing who you wanted your estate to go to, so they will decide who is entitled to a share in your estate. Hence, the beneficiaries they name may not be the ones you wanted to leave your estate to.

A will is a living document and should be updated at least every five years. You may update a will by a codicil, which is an addition, or a minor change to a will. You may not want to change the whole will, but perhaps something has come up and you want to add someone to your will or to take someone out. This is easy to do and often necessary. Who knows, you might outlive your heirs!

I know that many of you will have trouble getting your husbands to go to a lawyer to write a will. Men often have trouble facing death as the business transaction that it really is. This has always seemed strange to me when you consider that men will work most of their lives to acquire assets and then not follow through by transferring those assets to the person who can use and enjoy them. This

situation is common and I hope \
confronted with it will do whatev\
her husband to write a will. Some p\
of television shows, I am sure) that al\
write a will is scribble on an old piece of\
so, being of sound mind and body, do he\
etc." This is not the way to write a legal,\
You must do a lot of thinking about the cons_____ of
your death. You write your thoughts down on p__er and
then you go to an attorney. Don't spend $50 an hour
thinking in front of that attorney, do your thinking at
home. He will then put your wishes in legal language so
that no misinterpretations or confusion can occur at your
death. This is the only way to be sure your wishes will be
honored.

The person you choose to be the executor of your will
should be someone who knows a great deal about your
financial situation. Someone who knows where your
records are; who you do business with; and who lives
in the same state as you do. All too often wills are not
changed when people move and if you should die and the
executor is in another state the court may change the
executor and appoint one more convenient to the deceased's home. So, if you have moved out of state since
you appointed an executor, you should do something
about it.

Probate

If a will is the only arrangement you have made for
the distribution of your property (there are other ways
which will be discussed later in the chapter) then that
will, at your death, must be probated in a court of law.
Probate is a legal process which involves alerting the community that someone has died. Notification is placed in
area newspapers.

The executor of the will (one will be appointed by the
court if the will does not specify an individual) will collect any income due the deceased and deposit it in a special account for the estate of the deceased person. The
bills of the deceased will be paid out of that account.
The executor is also charged with finding out what all the
assets are and must keep records of everything he/she

...ne bills are in and paid. Then he/she esti-
... pays any taxes due and presents the records to
...ourt. If everything is in order the specifications of the
will are carried out. The length of time that this process
can take is indeterminate but can vary from one year to
many. Fees, determined by law, are paid to the executor
and the attorney out of the estate as well as all court
costs.

If the executor is the wife of the deceased or a sole
beneficiary, she should consider refusing the fee. This may
seem strange, but if you accept the fee, you will have to
pay income taxes on that earned money. Whereas if you
receive the same money (since the fee comes from the
estate) as a beneficiary, there may be no estate or inheritance taxes due.

One of the major concerns that many people have
about probate is that they will have nothing to live on
while the assets of the estate are being probated. This is
not so. The courts are aware of the fact that you must
have income during this entire process. The first thing you
should know is that any life insurance benefits are not
frozen. Death taxes may have to be paid on the money
you receive, but if you are listed as the beneficiary the
money goes directly to you. If you own the policy on
your husband then it is part of your assets, not his, so
no death taxes are paid. The executor of the will can also
petition the courts to grant emergency funds to the beneficiaries of the deceased. The courts will not deprive you
of an income from the estate. They just want to know
what the total assets are before any money is taken out.
This fear of all the money being frozen has caused many
a woman to do strange things. Every woman should go to
her bank and ask what would happen if my husband died
today? How much money can I draw from our joint bank
account? The more you know about the situation, the
easier things will be.

Now as I mentioned earlier, there are other arrangements that can be made that eliminate the need to probate a will. This doesn't mean you shouldn't have a will,
because a will is necessary in the eventuality that you both
die at the same time. But what if your husband dies first?
Depending on the way you and your husband hold title on
your assets (the way you own your assets), probating a
will may not be necessary.

Joint tenancy is one way of holding title that makes probating a will unnecessary. It is a common way of holding title between husband and wife and one that I strongly recommend. Joint tenancy is literally a will. It supercedes any written will and is irrevocable (unchangeable) unless consent is given by the party being deleted from the agreement. If your assets (real estate, investments, savings accounts) are held in joint tenancy, the surviving partner can handle all the formal paper work without an attorney. You may have to pay death taxes on the estate, but you do not have to go through probate. The assets are not frozen. They revert to the surviving member of the joint tenancy agreement after all paper work is in order. Joint tenancy is an excellent way to handle the transfer of assets at death. This is especially true if it is already understood between husband and wife that the surviving partner will receive all the assets. A written will would accomplish the same thing, but it would have to be probated, which is both time consuming and expensive.

Now you don't have to be husband and wife to set up a joint tenancy arrangement of your assets and it isn't limited to just two people. There are many situations that would lend themselves to setting up a joint tenancy agreement, but it is important to recognize what joint tenancy really means.

Where you can run into trouble on joint tenancies is if Grandpa puts his house in joint tenancy with his three daughters. He might do this to avoid probate, assuming that by doing this each daughter will get one-third of the farm when he dies. This is not what happens. What happens is that when Grandpa dies the three daughters inherit the farm together. If one of the daughters dies, the other two daughters inherit the farm. Nothing would go to the heirs of the deceased daughter. When the second daughter dies (if the farm was still held in joint tenancy), the third daughter would inherit the entire farm. Again nothing would go to the heirs of the second daughter. The last daughter would receive the entire farm. This is not what Grandpa wanted.

How could this situation have been avoided? Well, the most logical way would have been for Grandpa to write a will dividing the property equally among his three daughters. Probate, in many cases is the least expensive way to divide property equally and fairly. If Grandpa had done this, each daughter would have inherited equally with the right to leave her one-third to her heirs. But what if the farm had remained in joint tenancy at Grandpa's death? The three daughters could have immediately registered the farm as tenants-in-common. Each of them would then own an undivided third and each could leave her portion to whomever she wished; even to a sister.

I really think that joint tenancy should be held between husband and wife in most cases, but there are other situations where it has merit. I knew an elderly lady, Millie, who was having a love affair with a rather questionable character and I was concerned that he might dupe her into leaving everything to him. I didn't want to interfere with Millie's life, but I knew that it was her intention and heart's desire to leave everything to her only surviving relative, her niece. I suggested that she put all of her assets into joint tenancy with her niece. That way, even if she had a weak moment and wrote a will naming her lover as her beneficiary, her estate would still go to her niece—the rightful heir.

Another case in point is the story of Jean and May. Jean was about 60 and May was 42 and although they weren't related they had developed a close relationship. They decided to move in together and pooled their finances to buy a home. They talked about what would happen if either of them died and decided that they would want the surviving partner to have the home. The house was put into joint tenancy.

Now, I know of another very similar situation, but this couple didn't consider what would happen if either of them died, and the house was only put in one of their names. When that partner died, the survivor only received a very small portion of the deceased partner's estate. This was not what they wanted. Joint tenancy would have avoided this unfortunate situation.

Another way of holding title to an asset that eliminates the need to probate, is to list a beneficiary on the asset. This is essentially what is done with your husband's life insurance policy. Remember, if your husband owns the policy and you are listed as the beneficiary, the death benefit is not frozen in probate; it goes directly to you. This can be done with any asset. If you have a savings account at the bank you can arrange with the bank to list a beneficiary to that account. Then when you die that account reverts to the beneficiary you listed after the paper work is completed. Death taxes might still be due, but the funds in the account can be removed by the beneficiary without any problem.

I know this sounds exactly like a joint tenancy agreement, but there is an important difference. A joint tenancy agreement is irrevocable. You cannot take the other person's name off the agreement, unless they consent to it. This is not true when you name a beneficiary to an asset. You can remove the beneficary's name or change it anytime you want.

Before we get into specifics about other ways that title can be held on assets, I would like to discuss three very important factors: taxes, state laws, and living with your husband's will. The bug-a-boo of saving on taxes also involves death. I firmly believe that making a financial decision strictly to save on taxes is unwise and this is especially important when planning for death. Millions of dollars are paid to estate planners every year to assist people in setting up trusts to avoid death taxes and probate costs. In most instances it is unnecessary, and can be dangerous. The new Federal death tax laws have virtually eliminated Federal death taxes for the middle-class person. Often when an estate is put in trust to avoid taxes, the beneficiaries (wife, children, etc.) are locked into a fixed income that becomes inadequate because of inflation or other unforseen circumstances.

The new Federal Death Tax Laws include a marital deduction that allows you to receive one half of the estate or $250,000, whichever is greater, tax free. Prior to 1977, any estate over $60,000 was subject to Federal death taxes. For this reason many people were encouraged to make gifts during their lifetime since gift taxes were one-quarter less than taxes paid after death. Now gift and inheritance taxes have been combned. There is no longer any difference in the tax rate on gifts made during your lifetime and those left at death. The amount of money one can give without his/her estate being subject to taxes is about $140,000. By 1981, this amount will increase to $175,000. This is quite an historic change. It is the first change in Federal gift and inheritance taxes since the 1930s and it eliminates death taxes for the vast majority of Americans. When you add the marital deduction ($250,000) to the $140,000 that can be left tax-free, the total amount a husband and wife could transfer between them without paying taxes would be close to $400,000—a sizable amount of money.

The catch is that the marital deduction allowed by Federal laws is not automatic. Whether you can benefit from this deduction depends on the way that your state views the legal relationship with your husband. This simply means that if you live in a community property state there would be no problem using the marital deduction because you are considered half owner of everything acquired during the years of your marriage. What happens if you live in a state that considers your husband the source of all income? All income is considered "his." In order to be able to use the marital deduction your husband might have to set up a system of giving you "gifts" over a period of years. This is not always the case, but depending upon what state you live in you may have to do some advance planning to make use of the marital deduction. This is true even if all your assets are held in joint tenancy.

You must find out what the legal status of women is in your state. I mentioned the places where you can obtain this information in Chapter 8, but I will reiterate them. There is your state's Commission on the Status of Women; the League of Women Voters; the National Organization for Women (NOW); and the American Association of University Women (AAUW). Your state inheritance tax office is also a good place to get information.

Taxes

What about State death taxes? They are usually very little, and depending on what state you live in, they are determined in one of two ways. The first way is based on the total estate after all bills are paid. The total estate is taxed *before* anyone receives any money. (This is the same way that the Federal death taxes are determined.) This type of taxation is called State estate taxes. The other method of taxation is called State inheritance taxes and the individual heir is taxed according to his/her relationship to the person who died. The taxes will vary depending on whether you were a wife, a friend, or a relative of the deceased. Most middle-class widows will only have to pay

State taxes if they are able to benefit from the Federal marital deduction.

Trusts

One of the main purposes of estate planning has been to save on death taxes. One way that this is done is by locking up your money in trust, so that your beneficiary can receive the income from these assets, but not inherit the estate outright.

I know it seems strange (and it is), but this is how it works. If Joe leaves his half of the estate to Jane there will be Federal estate taxes due on it (remember, only if it a very large estate). Then when Jane dies, Joe's half which is now part of her estate, will be taxed again when she leaves it to their children. Estate planners advise Joe that he shouldn't let this happen and should set up a trust for his wife. Their theory is that Jane doesn't need to inherit his estate outright, because she will most likely never need to touch the principal. In theory this may be true, particularly if Jane is quite elderly, but otherwise it is a very large and sometimes tragic assumption.

I am very concerned for the woman under 60 who is expected to live on the income from a trust. No one considers the number of years she has left to live or the steady increases in the cost of living. Too many women who are forced to try and live on the income from a trust can barely make ends meet, let alone enjoy the comforts she and her husband have earned together. I am not referring to the family with a $500,000 estate or more, but the family with a $300,000 estate. This may seem like an enormous amount of money, but it's not. We are living in the past by not realizing the drastic changes that have taken place with regards to amounts of money. We still think $100,000 is a large estate when in reality $100,000 invested at a prudent 6 per cent will only provide a monthly income of $500. This is a pittance to live on. Before you let yourself get locked into a trust look at the size of your estate and think twice about it.

The truth of the matter is, ladies, that all estate planning books are written for men and by men. The first statement that you will find in these books is the fact (whose fact, I'd like to know!) that "Most of your wives, men, would not want to or be capable of handling their own funds." Inevitably, you will find other recommendations, such as: "Well, let's see, Mr. Jones, you want to leave everything to your son and daughter. I would suggest that you put half of your estate in trust for your daughter and that way she'll have a nice steady income, but won't have worry about what to do with all that money. On the other hand, I would suggest that you leave half of the estate outright to your son. He might need the principal to start a business or something like that."

I am not exaggerating! The assumption is that a woman is unable to cope with large sums of money. Besides, if you left the estate outright to your wife, she might remarry and then your children might never get any of your assets. She might give all of it to her new husband! In this case the estate planner might say, "Mr. Jones, why don't you put your estate in a trust for your wife and she will have income from the trust until she dies, then your children will inherit the estate intact and you also avoid double taxes!" God help us all!

When is someone besides myself going to stand up and scream that it is not "his" money, but "our" money! Let's talk about family money. A husband's contribution to the family income is easy to determine because he brings home a slip of paper that says he earned X number of dollars. But what about a wife's contribution? She's Sophie, the wife who never worked. It is impossible to determine her contribution on a monetary basis, but if you could, I think you'd find she earned *more* than her half. I think all wives and mothers should stand up and take a bow and say, "John, I did earn half of all we have acquired, even though I don't have a piece of paper to prove it."

So, why is it, that when estate planners come around, no one asks the wife what her ideas on the subject might be? Why are all the estate planning books written for the husband? Is it because everyone (men and women) accepts the belief that women can't manage money? Is that really fair? I don't think that being male or female has anything to do with intelligent money management. There are just as many men who do some rather stupid things with money as there are women, but it is generally taken for granted that women can't manage their own money. Yes, that's right, her *own* money.

If women normally died before their husbands, would we have all this estate planning? I rather doubt it. We assume that a man knows how to manage money. Does he? I know hundreds of women who manage all the family money and have to make a point to make sure their husbands know where all the assets are and how they work. Do those men feel that their funds should be locked up in trusts? Do they feel that they should be restricted to only having the income from one half of the family money just in order to save on estate and inheritance taxes? I doubt it.

Women may not have the same amount of experience as men in making investments or managing their money, but times have changed—all women are educated. More and more women are beginning to realize that finance is not difficult and beyond that, many find that it is an interesting and challenging field. After all, aren't women the family shoppers? If they are encouraged, don't you think that a woman might be able to do as good a job as a man? I don't just think so, I know so!

So the question I must put to you is, can you live with your husband's will? Truthfully, I don't believe that the average man wants his wife to be hurt, he simply hasn't thought about all the ramifications. You should make it your business to appraise him of these ramifications. All he has thought about are all the taxes that could be saved. Most of you can not afford to be involved in trusts. When you're talking about estate planning the first question you have to ask is, how much tax am I saving by doing this? Is that tax savings worth the amount of money it is going to cost to set up the trust and pay the trustee? It is not cheap to set up a trust and because of the new Federal tax laws, the trust could be more expensive than the taxes would have been.

One day I got a call from my friend Bertha. She wanted me to call her attorney regarding her investment account. It seems that he wanted her to make a name change on her account. I called him to find out what was going on. The change he was suggesting was that Bertha be made the trustee of her trust. It all sounded very complicated and was coated with some lovely legal language. I was confused by his story so I went to see Bertha to get her version. It seems that a friend of hers who lived in the penthouse apartment above her, told Bertha about this marvelous young attorney who was saving her oodles of money in taxes. So, Bertha, thinking that she could save money too, went to the eager young attorney. His great tax-saving idea was a trust. His advice didn't apply to my dear friend Bertha, whose small account only totaled $8,000. The cost of administering a trust would be almost more than the income she received from the trust. This is not good money management. Trusts are luxury items and must be looked at as such.

I would recommend that any woman whose husband is planning to put their estate in a trust try to stop him. Get out a pencil and paper and start putting together a proposal that would show your husband that a trust is unnecessary. Your proposal should include a budget of your monthly (and annual) expenses; your resources for meeting those expenses (this should be based on what your income would be without the trust and what it would be with a trust); and your age. You should also figure in an inflation factor (See inflation chart in Appendix). This inflation factor, even a conservative one of say 3 per cent annually, is particularly important for a young woman because of the greater number of years she has ahead of her. It's a common fact that people living on fixed incomes have been severely hurt by inflation in the last ten years and the trend does not look as though it is going to change anytime in the near future. I hate to sound like a fanatic on this, but I am firmly convinced that the average woman does not need her money tied up in a trust. Unless you are up in the $500,000 bracket, you have no business being involved in a trust.

There are no absolute truths in this world, however, so I must admit that there are some instances when a trust is just what is needed. What has to be considered is who is going to inherit your money. Are they minor children who will need care? A person who has never handled money and who will need a strong guide? Or is it someone that you know is a spendthrift? How old are they? What are their individual needs? Is your heir capable of management? How much money and assets are involved and how do those assets function? Is there an outside influence? All of these questions should be asked when you are writing your will.

I know a woman who wanted to update her will and

she told me that her problem was that one of her daughters was married and her in-laws were financially irresponsible people who were bankrupt by the time they were in their sixties. Her daughter's husband had allowed his parents to live in his home. The in-laws had even used some of the gifts and money that this woman had given her daughter.

In this case, there was an outside influence which made it wise to lock up a person's money. This way the daughter wouldn't be under pressure from her husband and the husband wouldn't be under pressure from his parents to use his wife's inheritance. We projected the daughter's in-laws' ages to 75, since they were both 60 years old, and proposed a fifteen-year trust for the benefit of my friend's daughter and grandchildren. At the end of the fifteen years she would get the bulk of the estate. We used the trust to eliminate a bad situation.

Up to now I have been discussing setting up a trust for individuals other than a spouse, but there are times when this is necessary, especially in the case of second marriages. My friend Nelly had married late in life to a widower ten years her senior with two teenage sons. She raised them and continued to work. Then her husband had a heart attack, so Nelly stopped working and stayed home to nurse him. When he died, she had been his wife for twenty-five years. She received the benefits from a $10,000 life insurance policy and some Social Security benefits, but the two grown sons received the house, which happened to be sitting on a very expensive site in the city. The two boys sold the house and moved Nelly out. This was a tragedy. In my opinion, a trust should have been established and the house sold with the proceeds from that sale going into the trust. The income from that trust should have been in Nelly's name for life. Then at the end of her life, the amount in that trust should have been divided between the two boys. This is how trusts are used to hold the assets until they can be given to others. Second marriages often need this kind of arrangement. When two people with a modest amount of money, marry, their combined incomes allow them a decent standard of living. But, if one of them dies, then hardships are created for the survivor. Why not keep their combined assets intact until they are both dead and then let the children from both families enjoy what is left?

Children

What about children? Legally, a minor child can not own assets. Their inheritance must be held in a trust for them until they reach legal age. There are two major ingredients involved in planning the futures of minor children. You need someone to raise them, a guardian, and someone to manage their money, a trustee. The guardian you choose for the child should be someone your own age. I don't think that grandparents should be made guardians of small children. A child needs someone who will be around for many years. Just because a child reaches legal age, doesn't mean he/she is ready to be on his own.

The guardian and the trustee should be two different people. Seldom is the same person right for both roles and besides you would be placing an unnatural burden on the guardian. If he makes a mistake with the money he will never forgive himself. Many people name a bank as the trustee for their children's funds and I think that this is an excellent decision. You eliminate any personal interest in the money. The bank must carry out the stipulations set forth in the trust and they are also responsible to the courts for all of their actions.

There is no standard trust. You can write a trust any way you want. The provisions of the trust are up to you. A trust can be set up for the lifetime of the beneficiary or for any number of years you wish. You can specify that the beneficiary is only entitled to the income from the trust or you can stipulate that they have the right to invade the principal. By invade the principal I mean that the beneficiary can use the principal of the estate as well as the interest. You can even define limits on the use of principal or the exact criteria under which it can be used.

A trust can be set up in lieu of a will or even in addition to one. Part of your estate can be held in trust and the other part can be handled by a will or joint tenancy or in any way you like. (It should be noted, however, that most trusts are set up in a will.)

There are two categories of trusts: those that go into effect at death, and those that are put into effect while the person is still alive. The first kind is irrevocable (unchangeable). The second kind is revocable (changeable) while the person is still alive, but unchangeable once the person who set up the trust has died. This second type is known as a Living Trust or Intervivios Trust.

A Living Trust provides for professional care of assets. Usually the person who sets it up is made the trustee and appoints a co-trustee, which can be a bank or an individual. Why would anyone want to set up a Living Trust? You could have a situation like that of an elderly couple I know. The woman, a doctor's wife, had always handled the family's finances. When the doctor became very ill the couple worried about who would take care of this sick man's finances if the wife died before the husband. They set up a Living Trust with the wife and bank as co-trustees. This was all well and good, but unfortunately when the doctor died, the trust became irrevocable. His wife was locked into the trust. The trust was intended to protect an incapacitated person (the doctor), but the end result was that the doctor's capable wife ended up having to live with it. You must understand how a trust works. Rarely do the parties involved in a Living Trust realize what happens when one of them dies. Before you sign be sure you *know* how the trust works.

What if the doctor hadn't had a wife and he became incapacitated? If he had set up a Living Trust with the bank as co-trustee before he became ill, the bank would have taken over the management of his finances. What would happen if he hadn't set up a Living Trust? Who would handle his finances? The courts would appoint a conservator. A conservator manages the finances of someone who is incapable of doing this for himself.

The conservator might become the executor when the individual dies. A conservator's fee is paid out of the assets he is managing and the amount is determined by the court. He/she is also responsible (as is the executor of a will) to the courts for his/her actions on behalf of the person whose finances he is managing.

As you can see, there are many ways that an estate can be arranged, but what really happens when a person (in this case your husband) dies? What do you do?

My first personal experience with death was when my father died. Arranging for the disposal of his body was probably one of the most difficult things I've ever had to do. No matter how prepared you think you are, when death finally happens, you feel like one great big exposed nerve.

When my father was dying I asked a friend who had handled her parent's funeral who I should go to. I called the funeral director she recommended and told him that my father was in the hospital and was going to die and that I needed somebody to dispose of the body for me. (This is rehearsing something before you get emotionally involved, because when you are emotional you cannot make good financial decisions.) The funeral director said that I should inform the hospital that his mortuary would pick up the body, and the following morning I should call and make an appointment to discuss further what was to be done. I was organized and trying to maintain control. I told the funeral director that I wanted my father cremated and he asked me what I wanted my father to go to the crematorium in? I asked how they normally did it, and the funeral director said that they were able to supply a box or casket. Well, I was prepared to go about this whole thing in a businesslike manner, but I just could not put my father's body in a box. It was the word "box" that I couldn't bear. So, I bought the least expensive casket they had. My father was very elderly and all his friends and family had died so the only people left who knew him were my friends. I didn't want any elaborate ceremony and instead I had a memorial for my father at my home.

This whole process of disposing of a loved-one is traumatic. It's almost impossible to be realistic about it. We have all heard the horrible stories of funeral parlors playing on the emotions of the bereaved. It's even worse when death is unexpected; we're caught offguard and everything seems to be happening at once. If you are unstrung by the death of a loved one, never try to make the funeral arrangements alone. Have a friend or relative go with you. Sometimes, no matter how strong you think you are, you can't grasp what is going on around you. Don't allow this to happen, get some help.

As you know, disposing of the body is only a small part of the death process. Now you must deal with the legal ramifications of death. It disturbs me that many able-bodied women who have been handling the family's finances for years, march right off to the attorney's office the day after the funeral. They never stop to ask themselves, "Why am I going?" Women have been programmed that they must go to the nearest attorney whenever there is a death. Unfortunately, thousands of dollars, money needed by many women to survive, have been paid out for the services of an attorney when those services weren't really needed. If the assets are held in joint tenancy between husband and wife, you don't need an attorney to settle the estate.

Truthfully, I cannot pre-judge the attorney who knows that his legal services are not needed by a prospective client. There is no way he can determine whether the woman sitting in front of him is temperamentally or technically qualified to close her husband's estate without the expense of his assistance. Fortunately, today, more and more women are asking themselves, "What legal services can I perform for myself? What help, if any, do I need from an attorney?" I have known several women who have saved themselves thousands of dollars in legal fees by closing their husband's estate themselves.

How do you do it yourself? The first thing to do is talk to a mortician. He can be a great source of information. He also has many of the forms you may need, such as the form to apply for armed services burial benefits if your husband was a veteran. He also will order any number of copies of the certified death certificate. You will need these copies to show proof of death in many of the financial transactions involved in closing the estate. Normally, twenty or thirty copies should be sufficient.

Next, you should stop by your bank and notify them of your husband's death. Banks are usually very understanding and will continue to deposit checks in your husband's name to your joint checking account. They will also usually let you withdraw money from that account after the balance has been noted.

If you have a safe deposit box, you will need to notify your local county offices. They will send someone out to be with you when you open it up and will make an inventory of its contents. Once they have itemized the contents, you will be free to remove them.

Next, you must contact your State Inheritance Office. They will give you forms to fill out and will also tell you whether it is necessary for you to contact the Federal Estate Tax Office. Whether or not you have to contact them depends on the size of the estate (whether you will be required to pay any Federal estate taxes). After you have listed all the assets and filled out the proper forms, the State will give you release forms for those assets. You can now go about changing the title on all of the assets. You simply remove your husband's name from the title. All assets will now be in your name only.

You also need to notify the insurance company if you have a policy on your husband's life. Submit the policy to them and tell them to please remit the death benefit funds to you. Be warned that the insurance company will most likely send a representative over to tell you of the alternative ways you can choose to receive the death benefit. These alternatives usually include receiving it as a lump sum; receiving interest only on the lump sum; or buying an annuity, which would offer you a lifetime income. Do not make any long-term financial decisions at this time. Wait until you have a clear picture of what your financial situation is going to be. You can always buy an annuity with the lump sum at a later date. There is no rush!

Another thing you should do is make an appointment with your husband's employer to check on any benefits that might be coming to you. Also stop by your local Social Security office and see if there are any benefits you should apply for.

The process is now complete. This walk-through of the death process was based on a joint tenancy situation between husband and wife for an average, simple estate. But what if it's a simple estate, but not held in joint tenancy? If you are the executor of your husband's will, the steps are basically the same except that you must notify your county probate department and follow any instructions they give you. There is no reason why you still can't handle the closing of the estate. The probate court will tell you if you need an attorney to represent you in court or for any other reason in the probate process, but basically, you should be able to handle everything yourself. If you handle the estate this way, you can probably pay an attorney on an hourly basis rather than getting involved with a large fee. You have all the information, so why pay a large fee to an attorney to have his clerk typist do the work you are quite capable of doing yourself?

The death process is not that difficult and from experience I have found that it is completed much more quickly, and just as efficiently if the woman does it herself. Most women do not feel like they can get on with their lives until all the details are finished up. They want to get their husband's death behind them as quickly as possible, so that they can turn the page and look to their future. There is no reason why an average estate cannot be closed within six months or a year at the most. The average length of time, if you go through an attorney, is now a year and a half. Why is this? Far too often when an attorney is handling the process it is set on the back burner for no good reason. It just sits there because closing an estate may not require the immediate attention that some of his other cases do. Don't let this happen. Find out the reason for the delay and if there isn't a good reason, harass your attorney until the job is done. Don't be shy or timid. You are paying him to do a job; make him earn his money. Besides if things are delayed too long, you may have to pay a penalty on State and Federal taxes. There is no excuse for having this happen.

There is an old saying, which all of you have heard and that is, "There are only two things you can be sure will happen in this world and they are birth and death." We've taken all the mystery out of birth, with everything from sex education in the classrooms to fathers in the delivery room, so why do we persist in keeping the facts of death a mystery? There's also another old saying—a Mary Roger's original in fact—"When a wife dies the husband takes her name off 'his' property; when the husband dies the wife inherits 'his' property." I want each and everyone of you to realize that there is no such thing as "his" money, there is only "our" money. Be financially responsible for your own future. Do not leave it to chance. Don't you be one of the millions of widows in America who are alone and poor. It's up to you.

Chapter Ten The Woman Alone

Most women who have gone through a divorce or the death of a husband need some time to adjust to this new chapter in their lives. It's not an easy transition to make, no matter how strong you are. After spending so much time living with another person, it's hard to adjust to the fact that there is now only one person to consider—yourself. In fact, most women have been trained to think of others first and consider it selfish to think of their own needs and interests. We've been programmed to serve others and put our own desires in the back of our minds. Well, now is the time to think of yourself and consider the things that make you happy.

The recently widowed or divorced woman will receive tons of advice from everyone imaginable. This advice is usually well-intentioned and you should listen to people, but hold off making any decisions for at least six months to a year if your finances allow you this time. You learn quickly to say "thank you, that's very interesting," when people offer advice and then store all of this information away for future reference. Once you absorb all of these ideas and determine what is most important to you, you'll get a better picture of what your future plans should be. And you'll see how many different choices you have.

Many women who haven't been previously involved with making financial decisions may find their new financial responsibilities are more than they can handle. There is nothing wrong in seeking help immediately. Go to a reputable accounting firm or the trust department of your bank and tell them you need *temporary* assistance. You're looking for help, in this transition period, to organize paying the bills, start record keeping, and to make financial decisions. Ask for this assistance and ask what it will cost. I don't want you to get caught in the trap of letting this temporary arrangement go on indefinitely. You should use this time to learn how to manage your own finances. Buying help, if you need it, is a wise thing to do, but to give up and not try to be responsible for yourself is unthinkable.

One thing you should be aware of is that a number of people suspect that a new widow or divorcee is a virtual gold mine. They imagine that you have received a large settlement or at least the money from your husband's life insurance. We've all heard stories of con-artists who prey on widows and divorcees, but not much has been said about the problems you might face with your own children and other relatives. It may sound horrible to imply that your own children might try to cheat you out of your money, but it sometimes happens without your realizing it. Again, I'm talking about the pitfalls of lending money to children.

If you've just received a lump sum of money your children may have some ideas about how you should invest it. They don't see any advantage to putting your money in a safe investment such as a savings account or government bonds that pay such low interest rtaes. In fact, they may be thinking of making an investment of their own—buying a new home or whatever—and figure that they can borrow money from you at a lower interest rate than the bank, but still higher than you would receive from a savings account.

This way, they think, you would both benefit from the arrangement.

No matter how much you care for your children and want to help them out, I feel that this is far too risky a venture for the woman alone to undertake. The actual transaction is usually sloppy at best, and the risk of misunderstanding is great. The best way to handle this type of situation is to say that you're sorry you can't help because you need your money for income. Don't offer any other explanation. No child under thirty can fully understand the needs and fears of the women alone. Don't expect them to. You need the loving support of your children at this time, but be your own counsel, don't lay the burden of making your financial decisions on them. You, and you alone, should be the decision maker. I'm not saying that you shouldn't give your children money if you feel you can afford it. Once you've found out what your financial situation is—how much it costs you to live, where your income is coming from, and how long it will last—then you may decide to make a gift to your children, one that you will be able to enjoy giving.

All you owe your children is being a happy parent. A parent who can make decisions without burdening them, a parent who is taking the responsibility for her own happiness, and who at the same time, can be supportive to them and enjoy their activities. This is the greatest gift you can give your children. The gift of not having to worry about you. And then at some later date when you get older you can advise them of your financial arrangements, but don't place the burden of managing your finances on them. The day you find that you can no longer keep track of your affairs as well as you should, go to a trust officer in a bank. This doesn't mean that you should set up a trust; you are merely using the services of a bank for record keeping and to assist you in making decisions. This is the smart thing to do because it isn't fair to your children to ask them to manage your money. If they made a mistake they'd feel terrible. Why complicate a loving relationship?

There are a great many advantages to being alone. You have unlimited choices if you can break away from old restrictions on working and living arrangements. First of all what do you really want to do? Perhaps the list of goals you once had doesn't make sense anymore so throw it away and start a new list. Depending on your age and how much money you need to live on, you have many possibilities open to you. You could be a firewatcher and live on top of a mountain, a waitress or chambermaid (oh, I couldn't) and live at the seashore, or almost anything that appeals to you. You can choose to live anywhere you want now that you're alone! When you are married you usually have to live within commuting distance of your husband's work—but not anymore.

Now you can do some of the things you've always wanted to do, but never had time for before. You could work your way around the world on ships, planes, and trains or drive someone else's car for them. You can work hours when other women have to be home, caring for husbands and children—at night, on weekends, or split shifts. Many new government agencies are beginning to divide jobs into two shifts. Explore all these possibilities. Don't place limitations on what you can do—if you want something badly, you'll find a way to do it.

Some women may find themselves alone—and without funds. You can sit in a corner and cry, or do something about it the way my friend Lillian did. Lillian was just about 70 when her husband died, leaving her with nothing. She had married late in life, and had no children. Unfortunately, she had married a man who gambled with high risk investments; he never invested in anything safe. After her husband died Lillian rented out one of the rooms in her apartment and became a chauffeur for wealthy old ladies. She would drive them around to friends' homes where they would be wined and dined. Lillian was paid for the driving and the wining and dining added to the enjoyment of her work. This job kept her going for years, even to the point that when her own car gave out, one of her clients gave her another car. Lillian filled a need and was able to enjoy life in the process.

Too many women limit themselves by holding on to the family home so they can pass it on to their children. There is no reason to stay in a house that no longer suits your needs unless *you* want to. If the children want the house, sell it to them, just as you would to any buyer. Most children don't really want the old family home, they just think they do. Try not to be too sentimental—if they want the house they'll find a way to buy it. Think of yourself first. If you want to keep the house, do it, but if not, sell it.

You should also learn to "travel light." Many of the possessions you own are more of a burden to you than a help. Not too long ago I realized that I had been holding on to some of my mother's things for almost thirty years, and more recently, I had acquired some of my mother-in-law's cherished possessions. I had been keeping these things for sentimental reasons, not because I really liked them. They were nice, but not exactly what I would buy if I had my choice. Many women are in the same boat. There comes a time when all of us should pare down our possessions and begin to "travel light." Why not get rid of the things you don't want? Give some of them to children and close friends, if they want them, and sell the rest. We all change and many of the things we bought years ago are stored up in the attic or don't have the appeal they once did.

There have been many times when I have been asked to help dispose of an elderly lady's possessions and it's not a happy occasion. It's so much better to give away your things to family and friends during your lifetime, rather than wait too long and miss the pleasure of giving.

Once you've pared down your possessions you'll find that you are much more mobile and can begin to explore different living possibilities. The cost of shelter today makes obsolete the old axiom that you should spend no more than 25 per cent of your income on shelter. It's almost impossible to find anything for that amount, unless it's in a neighborhood where you wouldn't feel safe. You might explore the possibility of sharing a place with another person. Years ago when we lived at the beach in southern California, I would see airline stewardesses living in grand old beach homes. They were able to afford some terrific places because two, three, or four people shared the cost of the rent. They were able to make their shelter dollars go further than most people could.

I think it is very important that the woman alone live as nicely as possible. It doesn't matter what the living arrangement is, whether she is living alone or sharing with another person, but she should feel comfortable in her surroundings. I have even supported a new widow's desire to spend 50 per cent of her income for an apartment with tight security, including several guards. After a year, her fears diminished and she was able to move into an apartment that better suited her budget. The shelter requirements for the woman alone should not be limited to a fixed percentage of her income. She will probably spend a great deal of time in her nest, so it is important that she feel comfortable and secure wherever she lives.

Many women make up all kinds of excuses about why they can't share a house or apartment. They wouldn't dream of sharing their own home with another person—think of all the valuable furniture that might get ruined or all the things that could be stolen. Nonsense! A smart woman should consider all her options. Living alone is costly and can leave you isolated from the world. Sharing a home is an ideal situation for many women, especially the woman who likes to travel. She has a built-in house sitter who can take care of things while she's away and the savings in shelter costs can give her the extra money to buy the things she wants and/or needs. You should explore different living arrangements and find one that suits you best. If you think you'd like to move to a new area you might consider renting your house while you take some time to explore the area and see if you would be happy living there.

Several years ago, an elderly woman I knew was offered a chance to move to the south of Spain. She was living in a senior citizen residence at the time and was approached by a con-artist who preyed on the elderly. As her conservator I was advised of her plans and stepped in immediately to investigate the scheme. I was able to prevent her move, but afterwards I felt very sad about the whole thing and wondered if I had made the right decision for her. What if Andy really wanted to live in the south of Spain? Why hadn't she thought of this when she was in her sixties, rather than when she was in her eighties? Don't wait forever to make your fantasies become realities. Take some chances with your life!

When Cam and I decided to move to a new area for our retirement our friends were aghast. "How can you possibly move when you've lived here all your lives?" they said. "All of your friends are here, your children—how can you do this?" Well, it's very simple. First, you rent a truck and load it with your possessions, then you drive it to your new home (or have someone drive it for you) and unload your furniture and that's that. "But what if you don't like it," they said. Well, you rent a truck and load it up and drive it back. The point is don't be afraid to make a change. No decision is irreversible.

As a woman alone you are bound to make some mistakes. We all do. Don't worry about them too much. There is an old Chinese proverb that says, "He who deliberates fully before taking a step will spend his entire life on one leg." Learn to be decisive, and if you make a mistake in judgment, turn the page and get on with today and tomorrow. There is a whole new world out there waiting to be explored.

Appendix

Annual Investment Required to Reach $100,000*

	5 Years	10 Years	15 Years	20 Years	25 Years	30 Years	35 Years	40 Years
4%	17,751	8,009	4,802	3,229	2,309	1,714	1,306	1,011
5%	17,236	7,572	4,414	2,880	1,966	1,433	1,054	788.39
6%	16,736	7,157	4,053	2,565	1,720	1,193	846.59	609.58
7%	16,254	6,764	3,719	2,280	1,478	989.39	676.08	468.14
8%	15,783	6,392	3,410	2,024	1,267	817.36	537.34	357.42
9%	15,332	6,039	3,125	1,793	1,083	673.06	425.31	271.52
10%	14,890	5,704	2,861	1,587	924.37	552.66	335.43	205.40
11%	14,467	5,388	2,618	1,403	787.41	452.67	263.74	154.84
12%	14,055	5,088	2,395	1,239	669.64	369.97	206.41	116.40
13%	13,658	4,805	2,190	1,070	568.67	301.83	168.00	87.29
14%	13,270	4,536	2,001	963.69	482.32	245.86	126.47	65.36
15%	12,898	4,283	1,828	848.82	408.64	200.02	98.68	48.88

* Due to the fact that there are many variables concerned in calculating compounding rates, these figures should be considered approximate only.

Capital Amortization

Amount of capital required initially to provide $100 monthly for stated periods of years assuming an interest factor on balance of 6% with all capital being consumed at the end of the stated period.

Dollars Monthly	Period of Years	Initial Capital Required
$100	10 (120 months)	$ 8,830
$100	15 (180 months)	$11,650
$100	20 (240 months)	$13,760
$100	25 (300 months)	$15,360
$100	30 (360 months)	$16,500
$100	35 (420 months)	$17,400

Retirement Data*

Monthly accumulation required at various ages to have at age 65 the capital amount

Age 25	Age 30	Age 35	Age 40	Age 45	Age 50	Age 55	of
$ 7	$ 9	$12	$17	$ 24	$ 37	$ 64	$10,000
13	18	24	34	49	75	129	20,000
20	27	36	51	73	112	193	30,000
26	35	48	67	97	150	257	40,000
33	44	60	84	122	187	322	50,000

* Table based on 5% interest compounded semiannually.

Capital-To-Income Conversion Table

This amount of capital	will give these monthly incomes at rates shown							
	3%	4%	5%	6%	7%	8%	9%	10%
$ 10,000	$ 25	$ 33	$ 42	$ 50	$ 58	$ 67	$ 75	$ 83
15,000	38	50	62	75	88	100	112	125
20,000	50	67	83	100	117	133	150	167
25,000	62	83	104	125	146	167	188	208
30,000	75	100	125	150	175	200	225	250
40,000	100	133	167	200	233	267	300	333
50,000	125	167	208	250	292	333	375	417
60,000	150	200	250	300	350	400	450	500
75,000	188	250	312	375	438	500	562	625
100,000	250	333	417	500	583	667	750	833

Monthly Amount Needed for Retirement

Annual Rate of Inflation	Today	In 5 Years	In 10 Years	In 20 Years	In 30 Years
3%	$1,000	$1,159	$1,344	$1,806	$ 2,427
4%	$1,000	$1,217	$1,480	$2,191	$ 3,243
5%	$1,000	$1,276	$1,629	$2,653	$ 4,322
6%	$1,000	$1,338	$1,791	$3,207	$ 5,743
7%	$1,000	$1,408	$1,962	$3,870	$ 7,612
8%	$1,000	$1,469	$2,160	$4,661	$10,063
9%	$1,000	$1,539	$2,367	$5,604	$13,268

Index

Abstract money planning, 25, 27, 32
Alimony (*see* Divorce)
American Association of University Women, 126
Amortization Act of 1934, 93
Arguments over money, 32
Assets:
  flexibility of, 63
  selling, 100
Automobile insurance (*see* Insurance)

Bank accounts (*see* Checking; Savings)
Bargains, 42
Barron's, 81
Bonds, 20, 22, 37, 43, 74–75

convertible, 80
corporate, 74–75, 130
discounting, 75
government, 72–73, 110
municipal, 74, 109
selling at premium, 75
unit trusts, 83
Borrowing, 41–43, 61, 84–85
  government, 72–73
  on insurance, 52, 58–60
  on real estate, 103
  and reverse mortgage, 119–20
Brokerage houses, 89–90
Budgeting, 33–34, 38, 122
  and divorce, 127–28, 134
Business insurance (*see* Insurance)

Business Week, 81, 85
Buying:
   necessities and luxuries,
      30–31
   speculative, 23, 70, 78–86
   (*See also* Investments)

Caution in spending, 29–30
   for necessities, 30
Charitable organizations,
   women and, 16
Checking accounts, 32–33, 39,
   42, 155
   checks cancelled, 36–37
Children:
   astuteness of, 39
   care of (*see* Death; Divorce)
Clifford Trusts (*see* Tax
   shelters)
Collectibles, 78
Compounding, 22
Computerized financial plans,
   22
Concrete money planning, 25,
   32
Consumer Price Index, 94
Co-responsibility, financial,
   14–15
Costs, hidden, 43–44
Credit, credit cards, 40–44
   "Average Daily Balance,"
      41
   and insurance, 62
   interest rates, 41–42
   "Minimum Payment Due,"
      42
   mortgages, 43
   sneaky business in, 41
   traps, 41–42
Crises, family (*see* Family)
Cultural activities, women
   and, 16

Death, 11, 12, 37, 139–57
   legal ramifications, 154–57
      attorneys, when needed,
         155, 156–57
      closing the estate, 155–57

men dying before their
   wives, 139
and pension plans, 37–38
planning and preparing for,
   140, 153–54
(*See also* Women; Wills;
   Trusts)
Decisions, financial, 15–17
Depression, the, 20, 21, 50
Discretionary income, 31
Divorce, 124–38
   affording it, 137
   attitudes, realistic and
      unrealistic, 124–25
   change of lifestyle, 132, 135,
      137–38
      budgeting for, 134
      finding a job, 135–36
      going back to school,
         135–37
   children, problems with
      and for, 133–35
   dividing the assets, 126,
      129–32
      cash settlement, 129–30
      family house, 130–32
   financial aspects, 13–14,
      125–26, 137–38
      alimony, 127, 128, 129,
         130, 131, 135, 137,
         138
      assets, money value of,
         131–32
      budget, 127–28, 130
      child support, 129, 131,
         132–34, 135, 137,
         138
   income:
      pensions and profit
         sharing, 129
      reduction of, 130–31
      Social Security, 129
      and tax statements, 128
   investment of settlement,
      135
   life insurance, 24, 57–58,
      128
   increasingly prevalent, 137

initial proceedings, 127–29
  drawing up budget, 127–28
laws, varying, 126, 127
lawyer, selection of, 126–27
statistics for women, 11
wife hurt most, 138
women's contributions to marriage, 125
(*See also* Women)
Documents, keeping of, 34
Dow Jones Industrial Average, 85

Education, children's, 21, 24, 28, 31
Elderly, care for, 24, 28
"Enemy," the, 15
Expertise, women's, 16
Extravagance, danger of, 14–15

False pride a nuisance, 30
Family crises, 14–15
Federal Depositor's Insurance Corporation, 72
Financial:
  decisions (*see* Decisions)
  goals (*see* Goals)
  history, family, 31
  irresponsibility (*see* Irresponsibility)
  isolation (*see* Isolation)
  planning, goal of, 53
    (*See also* Money management)
  plans, computerized, 22
  professionals, 23–25
Fire insurance (*see* Insurance)
Fixed income, 122
Flexibility in planning, 24, 25
Ford Foundation, 14
Fringe benefits, 22
Fund raising, women and, 16

Goals:
  financial, 20–27
  in life, 28, 31

Health insurance (*see* Insurance)
Health Maintenance Organizations, 66
Hidden costs (*see Costs*)
Home inventory (*see* Inventory)
Homeowner's insurance (*see* Insurance)
House, buying and selling (*see* Real estate)

Income(s):
  discretionary, 31
  fixed, 122
  husband and wife, 39–40
    saving one, 40
Incorporating, 77
Individual Retirement Account (IRA) (*see* Tax shelters)
Inflation, 21, 50, 56, 120, 132, 145, 150
Information, necessary, 23–24
Inheritance, 28, 38
  (*See also* Taxes; Wills)
Insurance, 20, 35, 37, 38, 46–67
  automobile, 47, 64–65, 66
    collision, 64–65
  bank accounts, 72
  business, 58
  fire, 47, 63
  health, 65–67
    "making money" from, 67
    national, 65–66
  homeowner's, 63–64
    renter's, 64
    and rising costs, 63–64
  life, 12, 24, 47–63, 156
    amount needed, 55–56
    annuities, 62–63
    assignment on policy, 58
    basic types, 49–50
      cash-valued, 49–50, 51, 52, 56, 58, 59–60, 63
      term, 49, 50–51, 52, 56, 57, 61, 63

borrowing on, 52, 58, 60
cash value of policy, 53–
  54
credit company policies,
  62
cutting losses, 61
and divorce, 24, 57, 128
double indemnity, 58–59
group, 37, 62
inadequate protection,
  51–52
minimum protection
  needed, 52–53
mortgage, 61
ownership of policy, 57–
  58
premiums, 38
  paying, 59
  waiver of, 58
price, 49–50, 51
probate, during, 142
reason for, 48
a temporary expense,
  52–53
traps, 59–61
  mail-order, 60–61
  "tax savers" ("Min-
    imum Deposit"),
    59–60
types of policies, 48–49,
  59–61
who needs it, 56–57
wife should buy on
  husband, 49
a money-making business,
  47, 67
overhead and profit factor,
  47
what it is, 46
Interest, interest rates, 41,
  42–43, 44
and bonds, 72–74, 75
and credit cards, 40–42
mortgages, 43, 99
Internal Revenue Service, 36,
  110–11, 114
Inventory, home, 38, 64
Investments, investing, 20,

22–23, 37, 40, 41, 44, 45,
  68–90
brokers and brokerage
  houses, 89–90
buying, 78–86
  collectibles, 78, 88
  investment clubs, 84
  on margin, 84–85
  options, 83
  real estate, 78
  stocks, 78–86
classic formula, 69
commodities futures, trading
  in, 88
loaning, 71–78
  banks, 71–73
  bonds, 72–75
  credit unions, 72
  to people to start busi-
    nesses, 77
  trust deeds, 75–77
in oneself, or family member, 88–89
risk, 68–69, 87
selling, 86–87
specific purpose, 70
speculative, 69–70
(See also Real estate;
  Stocks; Tax shelters)
Irresponsibility, financial, 17–
  18
Isolation, financial, 17–19

Kaiser Medical Plan, 66
Keogh Plan (see Tax shelters)

Land (see Real estate)
League of Women Voters, 126
Life insurance (see Insurance)
Loans, loaning, 22, 43, 71–78
  to friends and relatives, 44–
    45
(See also Investments)
Lump sum, acquiring, 39–40
Luxuries, buying of, 30, 31

Management of money, 27–45
  budgeting, 33–34, 38

and caution in spending, 29–30
credit, 40–44
hidden costs, 43–44
and life goals, 28, 30–31
loaning to friends and relatives, 44–45
priorities, 31
records, keeping of, 19–20, 31–39
small spending makes the difference, 42
Marriage:
  a partnership, 17, 25–26, 148, 157
  statistics for women, 11
  women's contribution, 125–26, 148
  (See also Divorce)
Medical expenses, 65–67, 121
Mini Keogh Plan (see Tax shelters)
Money:
  changing world of, 15–16, 21
  concrete approach to planning, 25
  credit, 40–44
  family arguments over, 32
  lack of, and anxiety, 39
  limited amount, 14, 26
  loaning, lending, 22–23, 40, 43
  management of (see Management)
  "penny pinching," 39
  stretching, 40
  waste of, 28–29, 31
Moody's Investor Services, 75, 86
Mortgages, 43, 75–77, 93, 94, 103, 108–109
  insurance, 61
  loans, 95–96
  remortgaging, 98–100
  reverse, 119–20
Mutual funds (see Stocks)

"My wife never worked," 13–14

National Organization of Women (NOW), 126
Necessities, buying of, 30

Options, 83–84

"Pass-throughs," 14
Paycheck, the last, 14–15
"Penny pinching," 39
Pensions, 12, 13, 20, 22, 24, 37, 129
  company plans, 110
  methods of paying, 37–38
  (See also Retirement)
Poverty level, 12
Professionals, financial, 23–25
  glib talk of, 25
  learning to talk to, 24–25
Profit sharing, 12, 24, 37, 129
Programming, past, 18
  need for overcoming, 15–17

Real estate, 20, 23, 35, 36, 91–105
  escrow, 35, 96, 97, 98
  house:
    buying, 91–97
      financial intricacies, 95–97
      location, 94–95
      modern mobility, 95
      paying, 93–94
      property taxes, 96–97
      remodeling, 92, 97
      retirement, 92, 93
    refinancing, 98–100
      investment, 99
    selling assets, 100
    selling, 97–98
      real estate firm advisable, 97–98
  improvements, 35, 103
  investment, 93, 99, 100–105
    apartment buildings, 101
    slum, 102
    borrowing, 102–103

capital gains, 103
depreciation allowance, 103
location, 100
non-liquid asset, 100
property taxes, 103
rental property, 103–104
researching thoroughly, 100–101, 104–105
selling, 102, 104
"land equals security," 91
reasons for buying, 92
title search, 96
Records, keeping, 19–20, 23–24, 31–39
basics, 32
budgeting, 33–34
checkbook, 32–33, 36–37, 39
documents, 34
family history, 34
home inventory, 38
inheritance, 38
insurance policies, 35
investments, 37
profit sharing and pension plans, 37–38
real estate transactions, 35
receipts, 35–36
Research, women and, 16, 20
Retirement, 14, 24, 37, 116–23
adjustment, 121–23
new financial status, 122–23
"retirement shock," 123
changing plans with age, 118–19
differing needs, 118
in foreign countries, 120–21
income for, 14, 21–22, 24, 28, 31, 39, 110–11, 120
reverse mortgage, 119–20
keeping finances flexible, 120
lifetime care, 120–21
and pension, 37–38, 110, 119, 122
relocating, 117–19

what to do with the time, 116–17, 122–23
(See also Tax shelters)

Saving, 14, 15, 20–21, 22, 28, 31, 39–40, 42, 43, 52
and inflation, 21
stable balance, 42
Savings accounts, 20, 52, 66, 72
certificates of deposit, 72
company credit unions, 72
equity in home, cash, 43
flexibility, allowing for, 63
investment, 69
and Keogh Plan, 110–11
and planning for expenses, 38–39
Selling, 86–87
assets, 100
real estate, 97–98, 102
Shopping, women and, 16
Social Security, 13, 122
and divorce, 129
and living abroad, 121
and Mini Keogh plan, 112
and planning for retirement, 22
and widows, 12, 55, 151, 156
and wives who do not "work," 13, 24
Speculative buying (see Buying)
Spending:
caution in, 29–30
small, 42
Standard and Poor's Investor Services, 75, 85, 86
State's Commission on the Status of Women, 126
State Workmen's Compensation Fund, 55
Stockbrokers, 86, 89–90
Stocks, 20, 23, 37, 43, 70, 78–83, 110
averages, 85
common, 80–81
investment clubs, 83

margin accounts, 84–85
mutual funds, 82–83, 86, 110
   brokerage fees, 83
preferred, 80
   convertible, 80
   cumulative, 80
price/earnings ratio (P/E), 85
selling, 86–87
splitting, 79
unit trusts, 83

Tact in feminine management, 17
Talents, women's, 16
Taxes, 20, 35, 36, 38
   bond interest, 73
   capital gains, 107, 108, 131
   estate, 57
   gift, 145–46
   income, 107–15
      alimony, 127–28
      (*See also* Tax shelters)
   inheritance (death), 38, 142, 145, 147, 149, 155
   marital deduction, 145–46
   state, 146–47
   mutual funds, 82
   property, 38, 96–97, 103, 104
   records for, 35–36
Tax laws, 16, 57, 113, 145, 149–50
Tax shelters, 23, 35, 87, 92, 106–15, 130
   Clifford Trusts, 114–15
   high-risk investments, 107
   incorporating, 113
   large-scale programs, 109
      limited partnerships, 109–10
   liquidity, lack of, 107
   postponing payment, 110–13
   reasons for, 106–107

requirements and understanding, 109, 115
retirement:
   company pension plans, 110, 112–13
   Individual Retirement Account (IRA), 112–13
   housewife's plan, 113
   Keogh Plan, 110–11
   Mini Keogh Plan, 112
   who needs them, 107–108
Trust deeds, 75–77
   amortization, 76
Trust funds, 28
Trusts, 147–53
   and children, 152–53
      categories, 152–53
      guardians, 152
      minor, 152
      and wills, 152
   forbidding expanse of, 149–50
   and increase in cost of living, 147, 150
      2nd marriages, 151
   and wife's deserts, 148
   when needed, 150–51
   and women as managers, 148–49
Truth in Lending Act, 41

U.S. Census Bureau, and statistics on women, 11–12

Vacation planning, 21, 31
Value Line Composite, 86

Wall Street Journal, The, 81, 85
Wasting money, 28–29, 31, 38
Welfare, 12, 57, 136, 137
   women one step away from, 11
Widows (*see* Death; Women)

Wiesenberger Financial
    Services Marketer, 82, 86
Wills, 139–46
    executor, appointing, 141
    heir, naming, 140
    making legal and binding,
        141
    probate, 141–46, 156
        income during process,
            142
        time required, 142
        when not necessary, 142–
            43
            beneficiary on asset,
                144–45
            joint tenancy, 143–45,
                155, 156
    and trusts, 152
    updating, 140
Women, divorced or widowed,
    158–64

adjustment period, 158–59
    temporary assistance, 159
advantages, 160–61
being adventurous, 163–64
being decisive, 164
children and money, 159–60
family home, 161
living comfortably, 162–63
mobility, 162–64
predators and cheats, 159
sharing a home, 162–63
traveling light, 162
without funds, 161
Women, statistics on, 11–12
Work, woman's, 12–13, 124,
    148
    importance of having a job,
        54–55
    research and planning, 16,
        20
World War II, 20, 66, 105